Auditing Bitcoin

Wiehann Olivier • Pieter Buys

Auditing Bitcoin

A Framework for Digital Asset Assurance

palgrave
macmillan

Wiehann Olivier
Applied Research in Management Cybernetics
North-West University & Forvis Mazars South Africa
Century City, South Africa

Pieter Buys
Applied Research in Management Cybernetics
North-West University
Potchefstroom, South Africa

ISBN 978-981-95-5774-5 ISBN 978-981-95-5775-2 (eBook)
https://doi.org/10.1007/978-981-95-5775-2

This Palgrave Macmillan imprint is published by the registered company Springer Nature Singapore Pte Ltd.
The registered company address is: 152 Beach Road, #21-01/04 Gateway East, Singapore 189721, Singapore

Foreword 1

We are living in a period where computing environments underpin digital bearer assets, reshaping assurance by requiring evidence verified at its source. In such systems, trust is no longer argued but deterministically validated, which demands methods that are scientifically rigorous yet practically usable. The approach presented in this volume delivers precisely that.

Grounded in Design Science Research (DSR) and operationalized through elaborated Action Design Research (eADR), the book introduces and develops the Bitcoin Audit Framework (BTC_AF). This framework translates classical audit assertions into blockchain-native, re-performable procedures, bridging the auditor's world of assertions and evidence with the engineer's world of keys, scripts, xpubs, and nodes. The journey from the Digital Asset Attestation Schedule (DaaS) through developmental BTC_AF iterations to the practical demonstration mirrors the eADR cycle, making the artifact transparent, reviewable, and repeatable.

What sets this work apart is its assertion-first structure. Financial statement assertions are mapped to concrete, independently executable steps. The "existence" assertion becomes recomputing balances from a full node at the policy cutoff; "rights & obligations" becomes demonstrating control through cryptographic message signing or observed address movements; "completeness" becomes deterministic address discovery (including HD/xpub derivation) and transaction harvesting; and "accuracy" becomes consistent fiat pricing and reconciliations to the ledger.

I write as a blockchain engineer who has collaborated on engagements across exchanges and financial institutions. In practice, this means building derivable address inventories, signing from cold storage on schedule, tracing UTXOs across periods to enforce cutoff, and reconciling on-chain data to the general ledger within acceptable tolerances. These are not theoretical ideals; they are operational procedures.

The broader context is equally important. Assurance becomes fragile when limited to screenshots, sampled proofs, or when "proof of assets" is mistaken for "proof of solvency." Empty cold wallets, balance leakage, and the masking effect of assets-only attestations are the predictable outcome of omitting ownership tests, address completeness checks, bidirectional ledger-to-chain reconciliations, and disciplined cutoff. A structured audit framework would not only have exposed such gaps earlier but could have reduced losses by front-loading ownership validation, ensuring completeness, and reconciling ledgers to chain data end-to-end. The benefits hereof are tangible. In one engagement, an ownership dispute stalled for days until the client signed a unique phrase from a cold key, our indexer recomputed balances from a full node at the cutoff, and the ledger reconciliation cleared tolerance within minutes. The debate ended because the evidence was incontrovertible.

BTC_AF also acknowledges that not everything is on-chain. It requires reconciliation in both directions: books to blockchain and blockchain to books. Practically, this means aligning harvested transactions from controlled addresses with specific revenue and expense accounts, checking cutoff with block timestamps, and validating fiat values with independent pricing at the policy timestamp. Fictitious ledger entries that never appear on-chain, and on-chain movements absent from the books, are unmistakably revealed.

Beyond individual engagements lies systemic risk. Digital asset custody now spans listed products, institutional portfolios, payment networks, and consumer balances. Blockchain-native assurance rooted in on-chain evidence, private-key control, address completeness, ledger tie-outs, and enforced cutoff reduces subjectivity in professional judgment and raises the baseline of market trust. BTC_AF offers that foundation.

For auditors, the framework is a program of reperformance: enumerated procedures, precise assertion mapping, and demonstrable evidence that reviewers can independently verify. For engineers, it is a blueprint for auditability: HD key hierarchies documented with derivation paths, deterministic address inventories, readiness to sign, and records that reconcile directly to node data. For policymakers and sponsors, it provides concrete language to define "good" practice, enabling requirements that mandate verifiable evidence rather than superficial reports.

This is a timely and essential contribution to both the crypto and audit professions. It unites the science of the artificial with the practice of assurance, translating protocol transparency into reliable audit evidence. Please read it with a practitioner's impatience and a researcher's curiosity. Then run the procedures, reperform the work, and raise the standard.

Sixpence
Pretoria, South Africa

Carel de Jager

Foreword 2

In an era defined by rapid technological advancement and the continued digitization of financial systems, the emergence of blockchain technology stands as a transformative development. Its impact extends far beyond the realm of cryptocurrencies, fundamentally reshaping how value is stored, transferred, and verified across global markets. Yet, with this transformation comes a host of new challenges, particularly for the audit profession, which is tasked with safeguarding trust and transparency in an increasingly complex digital landscape.

In this book, *Auditing Blockchain: A Framework for Bitcoin Assurance*, the authors bring a unique blend of technical expertise, practical experience, and academic rigor to a subject that is often misunderstood and oversimplified. This book is not merely a theoretical exploration; it is a pragmatic guide grounded in real-world challenges and informed by extensive engagement with industry practitioners and thought leaders.

At its core, the book envisions the development of the Bitcoin Audit Framework (BTC_AF), a structured, assertion-based methodology designed to address the unique complexities of auditing bitcoin-related balances and transactions. This framework offers auditors a clear path to obtaining sufficient and reliable evidence in a blockchain context. It bridges the gap between traditional audit methodologies and the new risks presented by decentralized digital assets.

The book not only discusses the technical underpinnings of blockchain and bitcoin, but also addresses the regulatory, ethical, and practical considerations that auditors must navigate. The book's structure, moving from foundational concepts to methodological rigor, practical demonstration, and critical reflection, ensures that readers gain both a comprehensive understanding and actionable insights.

For auditors, regulators, and financial professionals, this book is an indispensable resource. It demystifies blockchain technology, clarifies the evolving regulatory landscape, and provides a robust toolkit for assurance engagements involving digital assets. For the broader business community, it reinforces the importance of trust, transparency, and adaptability.

As blockchain technology continues to evolve and permeate new sectors, the need for informed, agile, and principled audit practices will only grow. *Auditing Blockchain: A Framework for Bitcoin Assurance* is both a timely contribution and a foundational reference for those committed to upholding the integrity of financial reporting in the digital age.

New York, USA Charles V. Abraham

Competing Interests The authors have no competing interests to declare that are relevant to the content of this manuscript.

About the Book

Auditing Bitcoin: A Framework for Digital Asset Assurance provides a pioneering exploration of how blockchain technology is reshaping the audit profession. As financial systems increasingly integrate digital assets, auditors face unprecedented challenges in verifying ownership, existence, and valuation across decentralized, cryptographically secured networks. This book responds to that challenge by introducing the Bitcoin Audit Framework (BTC_AF)—a rigorously developed, assertion-based methodology aligned with International Standards on Auditing (ISA).

Grounded in design sciences, the work bridges theory and practice through iterative collaboration between blockchain engineers and audit professionals. It presents the Digital Asset Attestation Schedule (DaaS) and BTC_AF as innovative artifacts that guide auditors through the complexities of blockchain verification, private key management, and financial statement assurance.

Beyond technical and regulatory insights, the book positions blockchain as both a disruptive and an enabling force within assurance and financial reporting. It underscores the need for adaptive audit methodologies that address fraud risks, evolving market structures, and emerging governance frameworks.

Offering a comprehensive synthesis of blockchain technology, auditing principles, and design science methodology, *Auditing Bitcoin* stands as an essential reference for auditors, regulators, researchers, and finance professionals seeking to enhance trust, transparency, and accountability in the digital asset era.

Contents

About the Authors

Wiehann Olivier is an Assurance and Advisory Partner at Forvis Mazars South Africa. As a Chartered Accountant (SA) and a Registered Auditor, he serves various clients, acting as the head of Fintech and Digital Assets for Forvis Mazars South Africa and as the global head of Digital Assets for Forvis Mazars Group. He has been featured in various South African and International publications, television interviews, podcasts, and online webinars for his expertise and thought leadership in the FinTech and Digital Assets sectors. Wiehann holds a Master of Science degree in Blockchain and Digital Currencies and a PhD from the NWU on blockchain-based digital assets. He has completed two executive programs: one on Blockchain Technologies at MIT and another on Artificial Intelligence at Oxford University. His experience in the FinTech, Digital Assets and Private Equity sectors includes consulting and assurance engagement services for VC and P/E funds, *en commandite* partnerships, digital asset exchanges, custodians, commercial banks, listed entities, OTC and arbitrage platforms, across-border payment and remittance platforms, traditional payment platforms and alternative asset investment funds in Germany, Hong Kong, Mauritius, South Africa, Switzerland, Sweden, Singapore, the UAE, the UK, and the US.

Pieter W. Buys is Professor and Director of the Applied Research in Management Cybernetics research entity position at North-West University, Potchefstroom, South Africa. With extensive academic expertise, corporate management, and consulting experience, he has assumed diverse leadership roles within these domains, spanning the manufacturing, engineering, information technology, and academic sectors in Southern Africa and North America. He is a Certified Systems Engineering Professional (CSEP) and a Certified Management Accountant (CMA), and his academic qualifications include post-graduate degrees in industrial engineering and management accounting. At the heart of his professional endeavors lies a dedicated research agenda, meticulously crafted to bridge the gap between academic inquiry in the broader management sciences and its practical relevance within organizational contexts. His research initiatives are deliberately geared toward making pragmatic contributions with tangible impact on businesses operating in the contemporary business environment, exemplifying a dedication to advancing knowledge and fostering practical innovation within management cybernetics.

List of Figures

List of Tables

CHAPTER 1

Introduction

Abstract This book centers on the transformative impact of blockchain technology, extending beyond cryptocurrencies to reshape financial systems and integrate them into diverse commercial applications. It focuses on developing a *Bitcoin Audit Framework* (BTC_AF) to address the complexities of auditing bitcoin-associated balances and transactions.

Employing a design science methodology, this chapter highlights key challenges faced by financial auditors, including private key management, fraud risks, regulatory compliance, and verifying the existence and ownership of blockchain-based digital assets. Grounded in *International Standards on Auditing* (ISA), the envisaged framework will aim to enhance transparency and stakeholder confidence in digital asset-related operations. The global evolution of blockchain technologies and their native and non-native assets will be explored, highlighting their implications for audit processes, regulatory oversight, and financial reporting.

By offering a validated and actionable framework, the envisaged BTC_AF will contribute to improved audit quality and support the responsible integration of blockchain-based digital assets into traditional financial practices.

Keywords Auditing • Bitcoin • Blockchain technology • Cryptocurrencies • Design science • Digital assets

JEL Classification M15 (IT Management) • M42 (Auditing) • O31 (Innovation and Invention) • O33 (Technological Change)

W. Olivier, P. Buys, *Auditing Bitcoin*,
https://doi.org/10.1007/978-981-95-5775-2_1

1.1 Background

Industrial revolutions signify transformative technological, economic, and social shifts that redefine industries, societies, and economies (Stearns, 2020). These historic revolutions may be categorized into the following:

- First revolution: Mechanized production powered by water and steam.
- Second revolution: Mass production enabled by steel and electricity.
- Third revolution: Automation driven by *Information Technology* (IT).
- Fourth revolution: Convergence of digital technologies and data-driven decision-making.

Effectively integrating contemporary digital technologies across industries, in line with the Fourth Industrial Revolution, requires a robust digital economy. This economy digitizes assets such as artwork, data, and currency, enabling the creation of blockchain-based digital assets (Yuan et al., 2021).

Over the past decade, blockchain technology has disrupted the financial sector and driven a range of business initiatives (Collomb et al., 2019). Emerging in 2008 with the introduction of Bitcoin, blockchain technology is increasingly recognized as transformative across multiple industries, including regulatory environments (Trivedi & Malik, 2022).

1.2 Contemporary Blockchain Technology

1.2.1 Protocol Fundamentals

Bitcoin,[1] the first digital asset to leverage blockchain technology, was designed as a *peer-to-peer* (P2P) electronic payment system, enabling direct transactions without intermediaries (Nakamoto, 2008). It operates on a distributed network of nodes that validate transactions, reconcile records, and ensure consensus. Combined with digital signatures and other cryptographic techniques, this process eliminates the need for trust between transacting parties and prevents double-spending.

[1] Note that for purposes of this book, a capitalized 'Bitcoin' refers to the underlying protocol, while a lowercase 'bitcoin' refers to the currency.

The Bitcoin protocol uses cryptography and a proof-of-work (PoW) consensus algorithm as its consensus mechanism to secure the blockchain, ensuring historical records cannot be altered without reworking the entire chain (Nakamoto, 2008). It functions on an open, permissionless blockchain, allowing anyone to run a node (Taskinsoy, 2019) while maintaining a full copy of the blockchain containing the complete transaction history. Certain types of nodes also validate transactions and blocks, maintain connections with peers, and enable verification of transaction history and wallet balances at any time (Palai et al., 2018).

Public and private key cryptography underpins the blockchain's integrity. A public key acts like a bank account number, accessible to all network participants, while its associated private key grants access to funds held in the public key, commonly referred to as an address or a wallet (Antonopoulos, 2017). A private key creates a digital signature by signing a cryptographic hash of the transaction data, ensuring only the private key holder could have executed the transaction. However, anyone with the corresponding public key and transaction data can verify the signature to ensure the transaction's validity. This means control over a private key equates to the *coins* linked to its associated public key, address, or wallet, encapsulated by the phrase, *not your keys, not your coins*" (Fröhlich et al., 2020).

Proper management of private keys is essential for securing blockchain-based digital assets. This is critical for individuals, investors, exchanges, and custodians to ensure security, accountability, and risk management. As a result, business models focusing on blockchain-based digital asset custody have emerged (FSCA, 2023), requiring financial auditors to implement procedures to verify the existence and ownership of related balances tied to addresses for assurance purposes.

1.2.2 Global Impact

By the end of 2024, the global market capitalization of blockchain-based digital assets had reached $3.25 trillion, comprising over 10,000 assets traded on more than 700 exchanges. Bitcoin alone accounted for over 50% of this market value, with approximately 19 million bitcoin in circulation, nearing the protocol's cap of 21 million (CoinMarketCap, 2024). Prominent US-based bitcoin mining companies Riot Blockchain (RIOT) and Marathon Digital Holdings (MARA) have a combined market capitalization exceeding $6 billion (NASDAQ, 2024), highlighting the scale of operations driven by this protocol.

Since Bitcoin's introduction and the advent of other smart contract-enabled blockchains such as Ethereum, blockchain-based digital assets have expanded beyond cryptocurrencies to include a diverse range of asset categories, which can be classified as follows (Bains et al., 2022):

- NFT tokens: Usually centrally issued, these assets are characterized by a digital representation of the right of ownership, making them collectible and non-substitutable.
- Security tokens: Centrally issued, these assets meet the definition of a *security* in the respective jurisdiction and operate within the regulatory parameters.
- Utility tokens: Centrally issued, these assets grant a right to a product or service, are accepted across multiple ecosystems, are transferable, and function as a means of exchange.
- Unbacked crypto assets: Usually decentralized and transferable, these tokens are designed to be used as a means of exchange, offering limited rights to the holder with no single issuer to enforce those rights.
- Stablecoins: Designed to maintain a stable value, these assets utilize stability mechanisms such as backing or collateralization with commodities, multiple currencies, crypto assets, or algorithms incorporating the backed assets.
- Digital currencies: Centrally issued by a state, central, federal, or reserve bank, these assets are designed to maintain a stable value, typically using sovereign fiat currency as the stability mechanism.

Globally, blockchain technology has become the foundation for various business models across multiple sectors, giving rise to *Virtual Asset Service Providers* (VASPs). According to the International Monetary Fund (IMF, 2022) and the South African Financial Sector Conduct Authority (FSCA, 2023), VASPs encompass a wide range of services, including cryptocurrency exchanges, brokers, NFT marketplaces, arbitrage services, digital asset funds, custody solutions, payment platforms, and cross-border payment facilitators. As blockchain technology advances, new business models emerge, further integrating blockchain-based digital assets into diverse operations. According to the FSCA's 2023 market study, most VASPs integrate unbacked crypto assets into their offerings. Meanwhile, central, federal, and reserve banks primarily focus on *Central Bank Digital Currencies* (CBDCs). However, this view overlooks the broader potential of NFTs, security tokens, and utility tokens across various industries and sectors.

Beyond VASPs, non-VASP businesses are also increasingly adopting blockchain-based assets to enhance payment efficiency and hedge against the devaluation of fiat currencies (Badea & Mungiu-Pupăzan, 2021). While blockchain-based digital assets have evolved into speculative asset classes due to their economic properties and market volatility, they continue to serve as a functional medium for P2P payments, maintaining their relevance in real-world transactions.

1.2.3 Market Dynamics

Blockchain-based digital assets serve dual purposes: facilitating payments, generating speculative gains, and providing digital representations of real-world assets. Over the past decade, methods for gaining exposure to and securing these assets have undergone significant evolution. Initially, investors relied on self-custody techniques but later transitioned to using cryptocurrency exchanges (hybrid custodians) or specialized custody solutions (Moore, 2019). Exposure has expanded to regulated environments, such as Bitcoin spot ETFs listed in Canada, Germany, Brazil, Australia, and the United States. These developments provide institutional investors with secure, regulated access to the asset class.

Coinbase became the first US-based cryptocurrency exchange to list on NASDAQ, offering services for sending, receiving, buying, selling, and securely storing digital assets. Similarly, OSL became the first digital asset trading platform to be listed on the Hong Kong Stock Exchange, further highlighting the growing institutional acceptance of regulated cryptocurrency exchanges in major global financial markets. MicroStrategy Inc., a non-VASP listed on NASDAQ, exemplifies corporate investment in unbacked crypto assets. It holds approximately 628,791 bitcoin valued at over $72 billion as of Q2 2025, with an average acquisition cost of $73,277 per bitcoin and an unrealized gain of $14 billion for the quarter. Businesses are increasingly adopting blockchain-based digital assets for payments facilitated by platforms like PayPal, which addresses the security challenges associated with self-custody.

Fiat-backed stablecoins, such as USDC and USDT, have emerged as a solution to the volatility of traditional crypto assets. Backed by fiat currencies, stablecoins leverage the unique features of blockchain technology to serve as a reliable medium of exchange. Initially developed on the Ethereum protocol using the ERC20 standard, stablecoins have since expanded to other blockchains with smart contract capabilities. By December 2023, the global stablecoin market capitalization reached $129 billion (CCData, 2023). Bitcoin has also integrated stablecoin functionality through the Taproot Asset Representation Overlay (Wang & Yu, 2023), enabling minting, sending, and receiving non-native tokens on its blockchain.

1.2.4 Fraudulent Practices

In the context of blockchain technology, the audit profession faces numerous challenges, exemplified by the large-scale corporate fraud involving FTX and Alameda Ventures at the end of 2022, ultimately leading to the collapse of FTX, the world's second-largest cryptocurrency exchange at the time, significantly impacting stakeholders in the digital asset sector (Schulp, 2023). Despite undergoing financial audits by the CPA firms *Armanino* and *Prager Metis*, the audits were heavily scrutinized by the *Public Company Accounting Oversight Board* (PCAOB) and the US *Securities and Exchange Commission* (SEC) for potential oversight failures and inadequate evidence (Lang & Gillison, 2023; Maurer, 2023).

FTX had a December 31st financial year-end and was not required to issue interim financial statements; it could employ off-balance sheet accounting for customers' blockchain-based digital assets and corresponding liabilities under *US Generally Accepted Accounting Principles* (US GAAP). This practice was later replaced by SAB 121, a regulation introduced by the SEC in 2022, which requires VASPs to record such assets and corresponding liabilities on their balance sheet for financial periods ending after June 15, 2022 (SEC, 2022). While SAB 121 was introduced shortly before FTX's collapse, its earlier implementation might have prevented this fraud by mandating asset reporting and compelling auditors to verify the existence, ownership, completeness, and valuation of the corresponding liabilities.

This case underscores the importance of regulations like SAB 121 in protecting stakeholders' interests by enforcing greater transparency and accountability among blockchain-based digital asset custodians. Compliance with such regulations requires independent, experienced auditors to conduct rigorous audits aligned with relevant standards, enhancing stakeholder confidence and safeguarding the digital asset ecosystem.

1.2.5 Governance Regulations

As blockchain-based digital assets entered the traditional financial services sector, regulators and lawmakers adopted three primary approaches (FSCA, 2023):

- Imposing a blanket ban, as seen in countries like China, Algeria, Bolivia, and Egypt.
- Proactively implementing regulations, as exemplified by Japan, parts of the U.S., Canada, the EU, and Australia.
- Taking a wait-and-see approach, observing developments before intervening.

Across all jurisdictions, regulators acknowledged the enduring nature of this asset class and its underlying technology, prompting the need to adapt existing laws or establish new ones to govern the industry effectively. These regulations often require VASPs to undergo financial audits in line with *International Standards on Auditing* (ISA) and similar frameworks.

Blockchain-based digital assets are typically classified as financial products (FSCA, 2022), which may require VASPs to adhere to specific licensing and regulatory requirements. These requirements may also mandate financial audits under the ISA requirements. These measures ensure comprehensive oversight of VASPs and their operations within the various regulatory frameworks.

1.2.6 Financial Reporting Requirements

As outlined above, many VASPs centrally issue and facilitate trading in blockchain-based digital assets. It may also act as a custodian, holding such assets on behalf of customers or investors. The impact of financial reporting on entities serving as issuers, custodians, and investors, as well as those receiving them as income or using them to pay expenses, is also considered (EFRAG, 2020). Accurate financial reporting is vital for all legitimate stakeholders who rely on transparent information to make informed decisions and uphold the integrity of the digital asset ecosystem (Smith & Castonguay, 2020).

Globally, companies must maintain accurate accounting records in compliance with locally accepted practices and prepare financial statements, which include the *Statement of Financial Position* (SoFP) and the *Statement of Profit and Loss* (SoPL), under guidance from frameworks such as *International Financial Reporting Standards* (IFRS) or US GAAP. Blockchain-based digital assets are typically classified as intangible or inventory assets under the IFRS framework (IFRS, 2019). Additionally, leading audit, tax, and advisory firms have issued guidance on accounting for these assets in alignment with such regulatory frameworks (Crypto Assets, n.d.).

1.2.7 External Audit Function Requirements

Global regulations mandate financial audits based on business size, public interest, entity status, compliance with legislation, industry-specific regulations, and lender or stakeholder requirements (Fiolleau et al., 2013). For VASPs, the complexity of their operations necessitates that auditors evaluate the risks of material misstatement under ISA 315 (Revised) and assess their competency under ISA 220 to ensure sufficient industry knowledge and expertise (Dyball & Seethamraju, 2021). ISA 500 highlights the importance of gathering robust evidence to support balances and transactions in financial statements.

While accounting regulators often provide treatment risk assessment guidance under IAS and United States Generally Accepted Auditing Standards (US GAAS), as well as various assurance frameworks, these guidelines frequently overlook critical issues, such as existence and ownership, in blockchain self-custody scenarios. As blockchain technology becomes increasingly integral to contemporary commerce, auditors must deepen their understanding to gather reliable audit evidence and ensure informed audit opinions.

1.3 Problem Definition

Blockchain-based digital assets have evolved beyond speculative trading by technology enthusiasts into a multi-trillion-dollar asset class integrated into the traditional financial sector. Businesses now transact with and hold these assets on their balance sheets for various purposes, necessitating regulatory and legal amendments. However, many auditors lack the knowledge and expertise to effectively service entities involved in blockchain-based digital assets, creating a knowledge gap that must be addressed to safeguard the interests of stakeholders.

Blockchain-based digital assets require auditors to possess specialized knowledge, expertise, and a deep understanding of the asset class, market dynamics, and underlying technology. Without this, auditors risk failing to identify and address unique risks, obtain adequate evidence, or detect potential material misstatements due to fraud or error, which can result in inaccurate audit opinions. The complexity of private key management and self-custody activities, especially in advanced VASPs that do not rely on third-party custodians, adds to the challenges auditors face in managing and mitigating associated risks.

Given the auditing and management complexities in a blockchain environment, the central question is how financial auditors can obtain adequate assurance at the assertion level for blockchain-based digital assets.

1.4 Book Objective

The primary objective of this book is to elucidate the development process of a *Bitcoin Audit Framework* (BTC_AF) based on universally accepted audit assertions, enabling financial auditors to conduct competent and effective audits of bitcoin-associated balances and transactions. In doing so, the book will highlight the key considerations for auditing entities with bitcoin-related balances or transactions.

This book adopts a systematic design science-based approach to attain the stated objective, addressing theoretical and empirical objectives. In terms of the theoretical objectives, the following:

- Elucidate the development of blockchain technology and digital assets, highlighting its integration into contemporary commercial activities.
- Explore the Bitcoin blockchains' technical and engineering intricacies and native tokens relevant to developing an assertion-based framework for auditing bitcoin-associated balances and transactions.
- Identify key aspects of audit evidence and its role in supporting the auditor's opinion by addressing management assertions related to transactions and account balances.

Furthermore, regarding the empirical objectives, the following:

- Assess and justify the design science-based approach as the preferred methodology.
- Engaging with the 1st iteration expert (practitioner) team, verifying and validating the actuality of the business problem through interviews with knowledgeable industry experts, resulting in the *Digital Asset Attestation Schedule* (DaaS) as a supportive artifact.
- Design a baseline BTC_AF$_{V1}$ grounded in the combined theoretical insights from the literature study and supportive DaaS.
- Refine the BTC_AF$_{V1}$ with the 2nd iteration expert (practitioner) team, thus verifying and validating a BTC_AF$_{V2}$ version.
- Demonstrate the audit of bitcoin-related balances and transactions using the BTC_AF$_{V2}$ to demonstrate the framework's practical *Proof-of-Concept* (PoC) application, culminating in the final BTC_AF.

1.5 Design Principles

1.5.1 Methodological Approach

The BTC_AF development will employ a design science-based methodology,[2] specifically integrating aspects of *Action Design Research* (ADR) and its evolved version, *elaborated Action Design Research* (eADR). Design science systematically creates and evaluates innovative solutions to complex problems through an iterative process of problem identification, artifact development, and evaluation. It bridges theory and practice by generating actionable knowledge to address real-world challenges and advance specific fields (Hevner et al., 2004; Sagor, 2000). ADR's iterative nature and focus on practical problem-solving have made it widely applicable beyond academia (Peters, 2009). Conceptualized by Mullarkey and Hevner (2015), eADR extends ADR by integrating technological advancements to enhance solution robustness and efficiency, particularly in leveraging information technology.

1.5.2 Data Collection and Knowledge Development

The overarching development process will involve designing and implementing various interventions to address the identified problem, moving beyond observation and analysis. This iterative process, a core component

[2] Note: Refer to Chap. 2 for the detailed methodological justification.

of design science-based methodologies, involves designing, implementing, and evaluating proposed solutions across multiple cycles.

The development of the BTC_AF focuses on insights gained through industry expert interviews. Thus, a suitable qualitative approach entailed open-ended discussions, allowing experts to share in-depth insights, experiences, and opinions, as suggested by Weller et al. (2018). This approach is central to exploring the complexities of financial auditing and blockchain technology, forming the foundation of the book's objectives.

1.6 Ethical Considerations

Ethical considerations are central to this research, ensuring the confidentiality and well-being of participants while complying with the Protection of Public Information Act. In line with UNESCO's (2005) principles on privacy and confidentiality and the *principle of primum non nocere*, the BTC_AF development process upholds the highest ethical standards throughout the research process. As such, the project underwent all relevant institutional ethical screenings, and the necessary ethical clearances were obtained.

1.7 Overview

1.7.1 Introduction

This chapter introduces blockchain technology, highlighting its significance and impact on the contemporary and future business landscape. It presents a real-world industry problem, underscores the topic's importance and relevance, outlines the objectives for addressing the identified challenges, and briefly discusses the preferred developmental approach.

1.7.2 Methodological Conceptualization

This chapter introduces the development and design methodology, including the assessment of the underlying principles of ADR and eADR, as well as the methods for data collection and analysis. As such, it underscores the scientific rigor of the developmental approach.

1.7.3 Principles of the Bitcoin Blockchain and its Native Currency

This chapter reviews the existing literature on the engineering, economic, and market aspects of the Bitcoin blockchain and its native currency. In this context, it aims to outline key considerations for financial auditors and identify initial auditing concerns related to digital asset balances and transactions.

1.7.4 Audit Principles and Blockchain-Based Digital Assets

This chapter examines the theoretical aspects of the ISA, focusing on the auditor's responsibility to obtain assertion-level assurance for transactions and account balances to support an audit opinion.

1.7.5 Problem-Centric: DaaS Development

This chapter explores the engineering, economic, and market aspects of blockchain-based digital assets. Engaging with the *1st Expert Team* validates the problem and integrates the relevant literature to develop an initial procedural framework addressing the problem statement.

1.7.6 Object-Centric: BTC_AF$_{V1}$ Development

This chapter integrates earlier literary considerations and elucidates the developmental process of the baseline BTC_AF$_{V1}$.

1.7.7 Validation-Centric: BTC_AF$_{V2}$ Refinement

This chapter focuses on refining the BTC_AF$_{V2}$, which is verified and validated by engaging with the *2nd Expert Team*.

1.7.8 Observation-Centric: BTC_AF Demonstration

This chapter aims to demonstrate the BTC_AF in a real-world scenario, validating the framework's practicality.

1.7.9 Summative Discussion

Chapter 9 concludes the framework development, reflecting on its effectiveness in addressing the problem statement. It will also discuss future industry developments, limitations, additional considerations, and closing thoughts, if applicable.

1.8 Summary

The rapid advancement of blockchain technologies calls for rigorous inquiry into their foundations and organizational applications. Beyond its role in transparency and decision-making, blockchain technology enhances auditability by providing immutable and verifiable records. This chapter positions blockchain technology within the frameworks of organizational performance measurement and management, financial reporting, and the auditing of related management assertions, demonstrating how blockchain technology reshapes governance and accountability. The next chapter elaborates on the integrative development methodology in line with the book's objectives.

References

Antonopoulos, A. M. (2017). *Mastering bitcoin: Programming the open blockchain*. O'Reilly Media.

Badea, L., & Mungiu-Pupăzan, M. C. (2021). The economic and environmental impact of bitcoin. *IEEE Access, 9*, 48091–48104.

Bains, P., Ismail, A., Melo, F., & Sugimoto, N. (2022, September 26). *Regulating the crypto ecosystem: The case of unbacked crypto assets*. https://www.imf.org/en/Publications/fintech-notes/Issues/2022/09/26/Regulating-the-Crypto-Ecosystem-The-Case-of-Unbacked-Crypto-Assets-523715

CoinMarketCap. (2024). *Cryptocurrency market capitalizations*. https://coinmarketcap.com

Collomb, A., De Filippi, P., & Klara, S. O. K. (2019). Blockchain technology and financial regulation: A risk-based approach to the regulation of ICOs. *European Journal of Risk Regulation, 10*(2), 263–314.

Crypto Assets. (n.d.). https://viewpoint.pwc.com/dt/us/en/pwc/accounting_guides/crypto-assets-guide/assets/pwccryptoassetsguide0223.pdf

Dyball, M. C., & Seethamraju, R. (2021). The impact of client use of blockchain technology on audit risk and audit approach: An exploratory study. *International Journal of Auditing, 25*(2), 602–615.

EFRAG. (2020, July). *EFRAG's discussion paper on the accounting for crypto-assets (liabilities): Holder and issuer perspective.* https://www.efrag.org/en/news-and-calendar/news/efrags-discussion-paper-on-the-accounting-for-cryptoassets-liabilities-holder-and-issuer

Financial Sector Conduct Authority. (2022, October 20). Declaration of Crypto Assets as a Financial Product. Press Release. https://www.fsca.co.za/News%20Documents/FSCA%20Press%20Release_Declaration%20of%20Crypto%20Assets%20As%20A%20Financial%20Product_20%20October%202022.pdf

Financial Sector Conduct Authority. (2023). South Africa's Crypto Asset Market Study. Press Release. https://www.fsca.co.za/Documents/Crypto%20Market%20Study.pdf

Fiolleau, K., Hoang, K., Jamal, K., & Sunder, S. (2013). How do regulatory reforms to enhance auditor independence work in practice? *Contemporary Accounting Research, 30*(3), 864–890.

Fröhlich, M., Gutjahr, F., & Alt, F. (2020, July). Don't lose your coin! Investigating security practices of cryptocurrency users. In *Proceedings of the 2020 ACM Designing Interactive Systems Conference* (pp. 1751–1763). Association for Computing Machinery. https://doi.org/10.1145/3357236.3395535

Hevner, A. R., March, S. T., & Park, J. (2004). Design science in information systems research. *MIS Quarterly, 28*(1), 75–105.

IFRS. (2019, June). *IFRIC update June 2019. Holdings of cryptocurrencies: Agenda paper 12.* https://www.ifrs.org/news-and-events/updates/ifric/2019/ifric-update-june-2019/#8

Lang, H., & Gillison, D. (2023, January 27). *U.S. watchdog should step up oversight of crypto auditors, say Democratic senators.* Reuters. https://www.reuters.com/technology/us-watchdog-should-step-up-oversight-crypto-auditors-say-democratic-senators-2023-01-26/

Market Activity. (2024). Nasdaq.com. https://www.nasdaq.com/market-activity/stocks/screener

Maurer, M. (2023, February 17). Lack of crypto audit regulation raises questions about PCAOB authority. *Wall Street Journal.* https://www.wsj.com/articles/lack-of-crypto-audit-regulation-raises-questions-about-pcaob-authority-a558754

Moore, G. (2019). *Custody: Crypto assets' unique challenge.* https://downloads.coindesk.com/crypto-investing/crypto_custody.pdf

Mullarkey, M. T., & Hevner, A. R. (2015). Entering action design research. In B. Donnellan, M. Helfert, J. Kenneally, D. VanderMeer, M. Rothenberger, & R. Winter (Eds.), *New horizons in design science: Broadening the research agenda: 10th International Conference, DESRIST 2015, Dublin, Ireland, May 20–22, 2015: Proceedings* (pp. 121–134). Springer. https://doi.org/10.1007/978-3-319-18714-3_8

Nakamoto, S. (2008). *Bitcoin: A peer-to-peer electronic cash system.* https://assets.pubpub.org/d8wct41f/31611263538139.pdf

Palai, A., Vora, M., & Shah, A. (2018, February). Empowering light nodes in blockchains with block summarization. In *2018 9th IFIP international conference on new technologies, mobility and security (NTMS)* (pp. 1–5). IEEE. https://doi.org/10.1109/NTMS.2018.8328735

Peters, J. (2009). Data-data: A model for practitioner-researchers. *International Journal of Interdisciplinary Social Sciences, 4*(3), 147–158.

Sagor, R. (2000). *Guiding school improvement with action research.* Association for Supervision and Curriculum Development.

Schulp, J. J. (2023). *Crypto crash: Why the FTX bubble burst and the harm to consumers.* https://www.cato.org/testimony/crypto-crash-why-ftx-bubble-burst-harm-consumers

SEC.gov | Staff Accounting Bulletin No. 121. (n.d.). www.sec.gov. https://www.sec.gov/oca/staff-accounting-bulletin-121

Smith, S. S., & Castonguay, J. J. (2020). Blockchain and accounting governance: Emerging issues and considerations for accounting and assurance professionals. *Journal of Emerging Technologies in Accounting, 17*(1), 119–131.

Stablecoin & CBDC Research Group. (2023). *Stablecoins & CBDC's Report.* https://www.ccdata.io/reports/stablecoins-cbdcs-report-december-2023#:~:text=December%2020%2C%202023,capitalisation%20for%20stablecoins%20since%20May

Stearns, P. N. (2020). *The industrial revolution in world history.* Routledge.

Taskinsoy, J. (2019, October 8). *Blockchain: A misunderstood digital revolution. Things you need to know about blockchain.* https://ssrn.com/abstract=3466480

Trivedi, S., & Malik, R. (2022). Blockchain technology as an emerging technology in the insurance market. In K. Sood, R. K. Dhanaraj, B. Balusamy, S. Grima, & R. Uma Maheshwari (Eds.), *Big data: A game changer for insurance industry* (pp. 81–100).

UNESCO. (2005). *Universal declaration on bioethics and human rights.* https://www.unesco.org/en/legal-affairs/universal-declaration-bioethics-and-human-rights?hub=66535

Wang, Q., & Yu, G. (2023). *Understanding BRC-20: Hope or hype.* https://ssrn.com/abstract=4590451

Weller, S. C., Vickers, B., Bernard, H. R., Blackburn, A. M., Borgatti, S., Gravlee, C. C., & Johnson, J. C. (2018). Open-ended interview questions and saturation. *PloS One, 13*(6), e0198606.

Yuan, S., Musibau, H. O., Genç, S. Y., Shaheen, R., Ameen, A., & Tan, Z. (2021). Digitalization of economy is the key factor behind fourth industrial revolution: How G7 countries are overcoming with the financing issues? *Technological Forecasting and Social Change, 165*, 120533. https://doi.org/10.1016/j.techfore.2020.120533

CHAPTER 2

Methodological Conceptualization

Abstract This chapter presents the *Bitcoin Audit Framework* (BTC_AF) design methodology. Grounded in pragmatic research principles, the envisaged BTC_AF aims to strike a balance between theoretical rigor and practical applicability by integrating empirical evidence and professional insights.

By adopting a pragmatist paradigm, the development execution aligns epistemology, ontology, and axiology to combine objective evidence with subjective auditor judgment, thereby bridging blockchain technology with established auditing practices. A design science approach will underpin the framework's development, employing design principles outlined in the *Action Design Research* (ADR) methodology. Per the *elaborated Action Design Research* (eADR) approach, enhanced iterations aim to address specific challenges through problem-centric, object-centric, validation-centric, and observation-centric phases, guided by principles of reciprocal shaping, guided emergence, and concurrent evaluation.

The iterative design process is driven by qualitative data collection, including semi-structured interviews with expert blockchain engineers and financial auditors. Thematic, narrative, and self-contextual analyses will extract meaningful patterns and insights. Verification and validation will ensure the BTC_AF aligns with *International Standards on Auditing* (ISA) and meets practical auditing needs, providing a robust solution for the complexities of auditing bitcoin-associated balances and transactions.

Keywords Action design research • Audit • Blockchain technology • Design science • Elaborated action design research

W. Olivier, P. Buys, *Auditing Bitcoin*,
https://doi.org/10.1007/978-981-95-5775-2_2

JEL Classification M15 (IT Management): M42 (Auditing) • O31 (Innovation and Invention) • O33 (Technological Change)

2.1 Introduction

This book aims to document the development of a *Bitcoin Audit Framework* (BTC_AF), which provides auditors with a systematic approach to validating audit assertions related to bitcoin-associated balances and transactions. Whereas the previous chapter provided the context of the BTC_AF development, this chapter introduces the design methodology, emphasizing its relevance to real-world auditing challenges, and highlights the methodological rigor to ensure the BTC_AF's practical applicability.

2.2 Methodological Justification

2.2.1 Introduction

According to Chen (2017), scientific advancement relies on rigorous, systematic research. Ensuring such rigor, Carr et al. (2018) identify the key principles of philosophical grounding, integration of insights and imagination, an interdisciplinary approach, systematic deductive reasoning for explanation and interpretation, and practical outcomes that enhance practices and processes. With various available methodologies, the design choice should align with the research problem (Turner et al., 2017). Wilson's (2014) honeycomb framework illustrates six interconnected facets that outline the essential components (see Fig. 2.1).

As illustrated, the framework comprises six key research elements encompassing philosophy, approach, strategy, design, data collection, and data analysis techniques. This structured progression clarifies each component of our approach, as detailed below.

2.2.2 Philosophy

At the core lie the philosophical beliefs that shape the scope of inquiry, guiding perceptions, and methodologies (Kivunja & Kuyini, 2017). In the context of this book, the philosophical underpinnings are detailed as follows:

- Epistemological paradigms like positivism, interpretivism, and pragmatism offer distinct approaches to knowledge development.

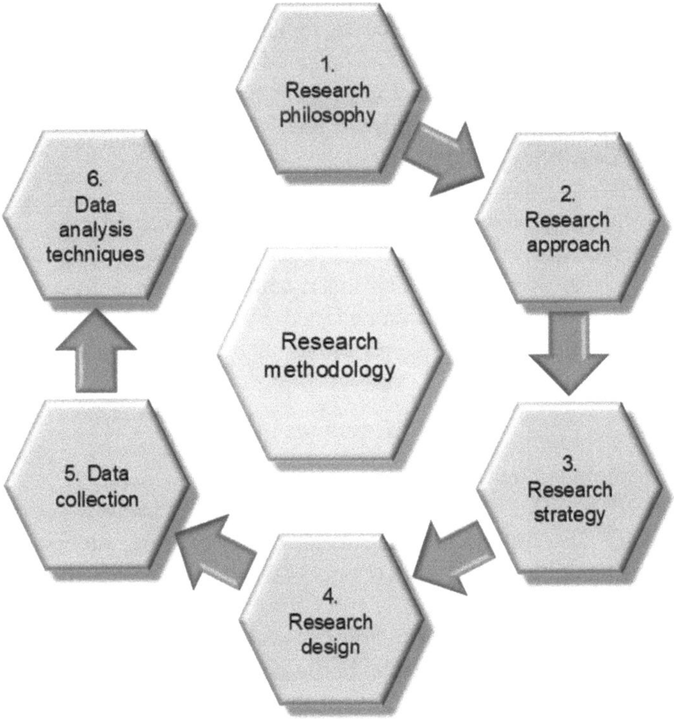

Fig. 2.1 The honeycomb framework. (Adapted from Wilson (2014))

Positivism emphasizes objective, predictive data through quantitative methods, while *interpretivism* focuses on understanding subjective experiences via qualitative methods. *Pragmatism* bridges these approaches, blending objective and subjective realities to address real-world problems with practical outcomes. This book adopts a pragmatic approach to developing the BTC_AF, combining verifiable facts and expert insights.

- Ontology examines the nature of reality, ranging from objectivism to subjectivism. The BTC_AF development leans toward *objectivism* in pursuing consistent, verifiable audit procedures, while incorporating subjective elements such as auditor judgment and practitioner input. Pragmatism integrates these perspectives, valuing *objectively* observable phenomena and *subjective* interpretations for a balanced BTC_AF.

- Axiology considers the role of values in research. Objectively, the BTC_AF design seeks unbiased, replicable procedures, while subjectively, it recognizes the importance of industry expertise and human judgment in shaping and applying the framework. Pragmatism unites these viewpoints, ensuring the BTC_AF is scientifically sound and practically relevant.

Adopting pragmatism as the guiding paradigm enables the BTC_AF development to address complex questions by valuing empirical evidence and professional insights. This balanced approach should ensure that the BTC_AF is technically robust and aligned with real-world auditing needs, effectively bridging blockchain technology and established auditing practices.

2.2.3 *Research Approach*

Inductive and deductive reasoning are fundamental research approaches (Wilson, 2014). The former involves deriving generalizations and theories from specific observations, making it ideal for exploring under-researched areas and generating new theories (Prince & Felder, 2006). The development of the BTC_AF adopts a *deductive* approach, aiming to establish a definitive set of procedures for auditing bitcoin-associated balances and transactions. Applying general auditing principles in this context, the BTC_AF will seek to align with established auditing principles, including verifying the existence and ownership of digital assets, and be grounded in *International Standards on Auditing* (ISA) while being cognizant of blockchain technology's unique characteristics. This structured approach should ensure that the BTC_AF is grounded in robust theory and translates effectively into practical applications.

2.2.4 *Strategy*

The strategy aims to bridge the theoretical frameworks and empirical investigation, ensuring coherent data collection and analysis to meet the objectives (Herek, 2010). According to Palinkas (2014), such strategies may include *quantitative* research that focuses on the statistical analysis of numerical data, qualitative research that explores human experiences and societal dynamics through interviews, workshops, and observations, and mixed methods that combine quantitative precision with qualitative depth to provide a comprehensive understanding of the topic under consideration. For the BTC_AF development, a qualitative approach is ideal for capturing the expertise of auditors and blockchain engineers. Workshops with such experts should provide detailed insights into professional practices and real-world challenges, thus aligning with the pragmatism paradigm.

2.2.5 *Design*

A design science-based approach will address the complex challenge of obtaining audit evidence for bitcoin-associated balances and transactions. Thus, it integrates research and product design, fostering innovation by creating artifacts to solve specific problems (Hevner et al., 2004). It employs iterative cycles, balancing the development of the design process and practical artifacts, ensuring solutions have direct applications (van Rensburg & Goede, 2019).

Rooted in the practicality of the design science paradigm, Sein et al. (2011) outline a four-stage ADR approach that encompasses (1) problem formulation, (2) building, intervention, and evaluation, (3) reflection, and (4) formalized learning. As indicated in Fig. 2.2, each of these stages further encompasses several key principles.

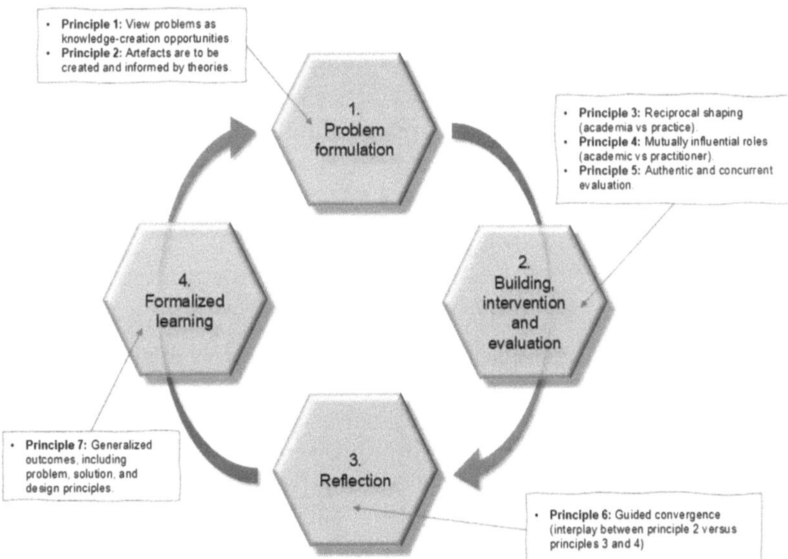

Fig. 2.2 Foundational ADR stages and principles. (Adapted from Sein et al. (2011))

This iterative process integrates practical solutions with reflection and knowledge acquisition, essential for developing validated artifacts. The indicated principles contextually align with the ADR stages, offering a comprehensive, cyclical approach that combines practical application with theoretical insight. Holistically, the principles involve validating the problem from both theoretical and practical perspectives, which also serves as the foundational justification for the researcher-practitioner teams working together in mutually influential roles to develop the envisaged solutions. This holistic problem-solving framework will underpin the design, verification, and validation of the envisaged BTC_AF.

Mullarkey and Hevner (2018) proposed further elaborative iterations to the foundational ADR approach, allowing various iterations to focus on phases in the overall developmental life cycle. In the eADR context, the basic ADR approach is therefore elaborated to encompass the following:

- Problem-centric iteration: Understand the domain of the problem and its connection to the business problem.
- Object-centric iteration: Focus on designing a baseline BTC_AF_{v1}.
- Validation-centric: Refine, verify, and validate the BTC_AF_{v2}.
- Observation-centric: Demonstrate the BTC_AF application in a test case scenario.

For purposes of the BTC_AF development, the integrated ADR/eADR iterations are illustrated in Fig. 2.3.

Such an approach should ensure a systematic, rigorous, and tailored development process aligned with the book's objectives.

2.2.6 Data Collection

Data collection is a multifaceted process that involves interviews, questionnaires, observations, and reviews of secondary data. Guided by pragmatism, this book employed a qualitative approach to data collection through interviews, as proposed by Abedi et al. (2019), to effectively address complex issues in a rapidly evolving technological context. Semi-structured interviews were particularly suitable in context, combining structured guidance with the flexibility to explore more profound insights.

- Team considerations: A *mini*-Delphi technique will be followed, and a panel of industry experts will be selected based on predefined crite-

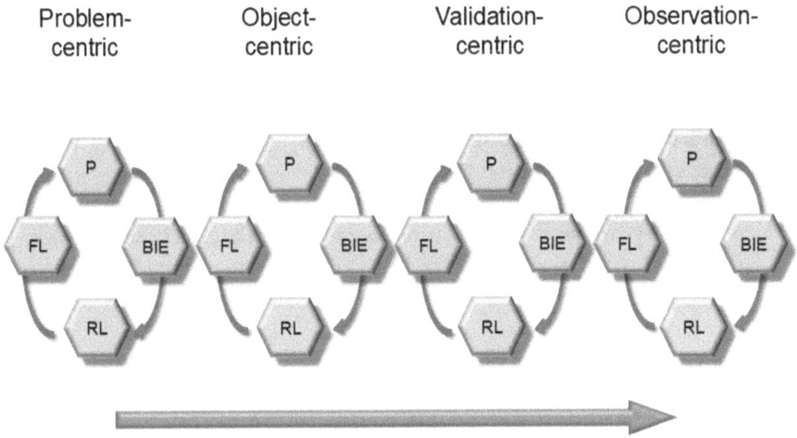

Fig. 2.3 BTC_AF development iterations. (Adapted from Sein et al. (2011); Mullarkey and Hevner (2018))

ria to provide informed opinions through structured surveys, questionnaires, or interviews per Fish and Busby (1996). The iterative approach emphasized structured feedback and diverse perspectives, as suggested by De Loë et al. (2016). Engaging with industry experts enabled the development process to delve deeper into the blockchain phenomenon, allowing for a comprehensive identification and understanding of the underlying realities. The industry experts will include blockchain engineers and financial auditors with experience in VASPs and non-VASPs, aligning with the book's objectives.

- Team composition: The BTC_AF's development, verification, and validation rely on iterative collaboration with industry expert teams. While the participant pool is somewhat limited due to the specialist knowledge requirement, expert insights and expertise remain critical to the framework's refinement. The following expert team compositions were compiled:

- *1st Expert Team:*

- Blockchain Engineer with expertise in leading technical advancements in mobile commerce, established a leading cryptocurrency exchange in Africa, and a company offering cryptocurrency transaction services for retail applications.

- Certified Public Accountant (CPA) and US-based Assurance Partner with 25+ years at a global international auditing firm, with expertise in auditing alternative investment funds, including those involving blockchain-based digital assets.
- Chartered Accountant (CA) and UK-based Financial Services Lead with 30 years at a global auditing firm, with expertise in leading complex regulatory projects and risk management for multinational banks.

- *2nd Expert Team:*

- CPA and US-based Assurance Partner with 20 years at a global auditing firm, with expertise in specialist auditing strategies for asset management and broker-dealers, including digital assets.
- CA and South African-based Assurance Senior Manager with over 10 years at a global auditing firm, with audit expertise on VASPs/non-VASPs leveraging blockchain-based digital assets for transactions and custody.
- Blockchain Engineer and CEO of a blockchain engineering firm, advising major institutions on compliance and innovation in digital assets, with expertise in conducting professional training across sectors, including digital asset auditing tools.

Interactions with industry experts, guided by literature-based questionnaires, will endeavor to clarify the contextual problem and objectives, providing deeper insights into the data. Sharing background knowledge will be limited to minimize research bias and encourage unrestrained expert contributions.

2.2.7 Data Analysis Techniques

The BTC_AF development focuses on qualitative data collection, capturing the industry experts' understanding and the interpretations they attach to the complex issue of blockchain-based digital asset balances and transactions (Polkinghorne, 2010). Hong and Cross Francis (2020) emphasize the suitability of qualitative research for exploring complex constructs and lived experiences in diverse contexts. Zelčāne and Pipere (2023) suggest that combining multiple qualitative methods and data analysis techniques enhances understanding within a specific context. For this book, the following is noted:

- Thematic analysis provides contextual insights into real-world problems by identifying patterns and themes in the data (Saunders et al., 2023).
- Narrative analysis interprets how individuals use stories to construct meaning (Murray, 2015).
- Self-context analysis examines individuals' roles and identities within specific contexts (Galliher et al., 2017).

This book will employ thematic analysis as its primary data analysis method, supported by narrative and self-contextual analyses. These analyses should be well-suited for semi-structured data and capture nuanced insights to develop a robust BTC_AF.

2.3 Methodological Rigor

2.3.1 Development Roadmap

Multiple workshop sessions will be conducted with industry experts. Initial workshops will introduce the objectives through insights from the experts' experiences. In terms of the timing and scope of the workshops, the following team structures are noted:

- The *1st Expert Team* will be engaged in the problem-centric iteration, primarily validating the real-world issue of auditing blockchain-based digital assets. This will result in the *Digital Asset Assertion Schedule* (DaaS) as foundational knowledge in designing the BTC_AF_{v1} baseline artifact.
- The *2nd Expert Team* will be engaged in the validation-centric iteration, with the primary objective of artifact verification, validation, and refinement. This will result in the BTC_AF_{v2} artifact, intended for proof-of-concept demonstration purposes.

The overall development roadmap is illustrated in Fig. 2.4.

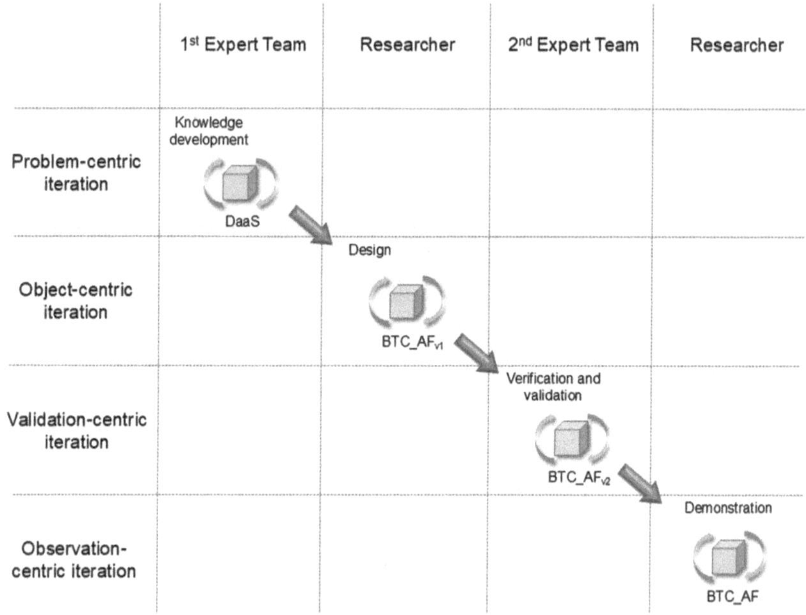

Fig. 2.4 Development roadmap

As indicated, the development process will result in three supportive artifacts: the DaaS, BTC_AF_{v1}, and BTC_AF_{v2}, culminating in a proof-of-concept demonstration of the BTC_AF.

2.3.2 *Verification and Validation*

The development of artifacts in the design sciences is a central component of this initiative. These artifacts, representing new practices and capabilities, are iteratively developed and should be evaluated to ensure practical applicability (Gregor & Hevner, 2013). The envisaged BTC_AF will incorporate the iterative flexibility of eADR to adapt to emerging insights or challenges. However, to ensure compliance with a pragmatic design science paradigm, it remains subject to verification and validation considerations to meet design requirements and address the business problem as experienced.

In terms of verification, the following design statements will ensure that the envisaged BTC_AF aligns with the requisite design requirements, focusing on key audit assertions as follows:

- Existence: Evidence confirms bitcoin balances exist with a custodian or on-chain at addresses controlled by management.
- Rights and obligations: Evidence that management holds a legally enforceable right to the bitcoin held with a custodian or their knowledge of the private key controlling the address where the bitcoin resides.
- Completeness: Supporting evidence ensures that all reported blockchain-based addresses and related transactions are accounted for in the SoFP and SoPL.
- Accuracy and valuation: Evidence confirms that bitcoin-related balances and transactions are accurately measured and assessed for impairment if recorded at cost.
- Cut-off: Evidence verifies that blockchain-related transactions are recorded in the correct financial period.
- Occurrence: Evidence confirms that blockchain-related payments or receipts, as recorded in the accounting records, are recorded on the blockchain.

In terms of validation, the following design statements confirm that the envisaged BTC_AF effectively addresses the research problem and meets auditors' practical requirements:

- Auditors can interpret and apply the BTC_AF to ensure audit execution meets sufficient and reliable evidence requirements, considering the complexities of the Bitcoin blockchain's engineering, architecture, and market dynamics.
- Auditors can apply the BTC_AF to obtain assurance over management's assertions on bitcoin-related balances and transactions in financial statements, supporting the audit opinion.
- Auditors can utilize the BTC_AF as a systematic audit program to ensure sufficient assurance over management's assertions regarding bitcoin balances on the SoFP and related transactions in the SoPL.

By incorporating these principles, the BTC_AF will be iteratively refined to ensure a robust, valid solution for auditing blockchain-based digital assets.

2.4 Summary

This chapter outlined the research design methodology, structured around the honeycomb framework. The underlying design philosophy is rooted in pragmatism, objectivism, and a value-free stance across epistemology, ontology, and axiology. A deductive approach and qualitative strategy have been adopted, supported by an iterative design science framework to bridge theory and practice in auditing bitcoin-associated balances and transactions. Data collection will involve semi-structured interviews in a workshop setting, facilitating in-depth engagement with industry experts to develop and refine the respective DaaS and various BTC_AF versions. Thematic analysis has been selected as the primary method of data analysis. The next chapter will focus on the intricacies of Bitcoin's blockchain technology and its underlying protocols.

References

Abedi, F., Zeleznikow, J., & Brien, C. (2019). Developing regulatory standards for the concept of security in online dispute resolution systems. *Computer Law & Security Review, 35*(5), 105328.

Carr, G., Loucks, D. P., & Blöschl, G. (2018). Gaining insight into interdisciplinary research and education programmes: A framework for evaluation. *Research Policy, 47*(1), 35–48.

Chen, C. (2017). Science mapping: A systematic review of the literature. *Journal of Data and Information Science, 2*(2), 1–40.

De Loë, R. C., Melnychuk, N., Murray, D., & Plummer, R. (2016). Advancing the state of policy Delphi practice: A systematic review evaluating methodological evolution, innovation, and opportunities. *Technological Forecasting and Social Change, 104*, 78–88.

Fish, L. S., & Busby, D. M. (1996). The Delphi method. In D. H. Sprenkle & F. P. Piercy (Eds.), *Research methods in family therapy* (pp. 469–482). Guildford Press.

Galliher, R. V., McLean, K. C., & Syed, M. (2017). An integrated developmental model for studying identity content in context. *Developmental Psychology, 53*(11), 2011–2022.

Gregor, S., & Hevner, A. R. (2013). Positioning and presenting design science research for maximum impact. *MIS Quarterly, 37*(2), 337–355.

Herek, G. (2010). Developing a theoretical framework and rationale for a research proposal. In W. Pequegnat, E. Stover, & C. Boyce (Eds.), *How to write a successful research grant application* (pp. 137–145). Springer. https://doi.org/10.1007/978-1-4419-1454-5_12

Hevner, A. R., March, S. T., & Park, J. (2004). Design science in information systems research. *MIS Quarterly, 28*(1), 75–105.

Hong, J., & Cross Francis, D. (2020). Unpacking complex phenomena through qualitative inquiry: The case of teacher identity research. *Journal of Mindfulness and Environment, 55*(4), 208–219. https://doi.org/10.1080/00461520.2020.1783265

Kivunja, C., & Kuyini, A. B. (2017). Understanding and applying research paradigms in educational contexts. *International Journal of Higher Education, 6*(5), 26–41. https://doi.org/10.5430/ijhe.v6n5p26

Mullarkey, M. T., & Hevner, A. R. (2018). An elaborated action design research process model. *European Journal of Information Systems, 28*(1), 6–20.

Murray, M. (2015). Narrative psychology. In J. A. Smith (Ed.), *Qualitative psychology: A practical guide to research methods* (3rd ed., pp. 85–107). Sage.

Palinkas, L. A. (2014). Qualitative and mixed methods in mental health services and implementation research. *Journal of Clinical Child & Adolescent Psychology, 43*(6), 851–861.

Polkinghorne, D. E. (2010). Qualitative research. In J. C. Thomas & M. Hersen (Eds.), *Handbook of clinical psychology competencies* (pp. 425–456). Springer.

Prince, M. J., & Felder, R. M. (2006). Inductive teaching and learning methods: Definitions, comparisons, and research bases. *Journal of Engineering Education, 95*(2), 123–138.

Saunders, C. H., Sierpe, A., Von Plessen, C., Kennedy, A. M., Leviton, L. C., Bernstein, S. L., & Leyenaar, J. K. (2023). Practical thematic analysis: A guide for multidisciplinary health services research teams engaging in qualitative analysis. *BMJ, 381*, e074256. https://doi.org/10.1136/bmj-2022-074256

Sein, M. K., Henfridsson, O., Purao, S., Rossi, M., & Lindgren, R. (2011). Action design research. *MIS Quarterly, 35*(1), 37–56.

Turner, S. F., Cardinal, L. B., & Burton, R. M. (2017). Research design for mixed methods: A triangulation-based framework and roadmap. *Organizational Research Methods, 20*(2), 243–267.

Van Rensburg, J. J., & Goede, R. (2019). A model for improving knowledge generation in design science research through reflective practice. *Electronic Journal of Business Research Methods, 17*(4), 192–211.

Wilson, J. (2014). *Essentials of business research: A guide to doing your research project.* Sage.

Zelčāne, E., & Pipere, A. (2023). Finding a path in a methodological jungle: A qualitative research of resilience. *International Journal of Qualitative Studies on Health and Well-Being, 18*(1), 2164948. https://doi.org/10.1080/17482631.2023.2164948

CHAPTER 3

Principles of Blockchain Protocols

Abstract This chapter examines the foundational technological principles, architecture, and dynamics of the Bitcoin blockchain and its native currency to inform the development of a *Bitcoin Audit Framework* (BTC_AF). It explores critical audit considerations for bitcoin-associated transactions and balances, highlighting the Bitcoin blockchain's decentralized nature. This blockchain operates without intermediaries and relies on cryptographic principles and consensus mechanisms, such as *proof-of-work* (PoW), to ensure security, transparency, and resilience.

Key components, including transaction processing and wallet management, are analyzed, with a focus on their implications for audit evidence. Furthermore, the role of mining in maintaining network integrity is explored, addressing challenges related to a blockchain's scalability, security, and decentralization. Advanced cryptographic features are introduced as critical tools for enhancing transaction security and enabling auditors to verify ownership and ensure data reliability. The analysis highlights the economic complexities of auditing bitcoin-associated balances and transactions. These complexities are driven by global, continuous trading and market volatility, which necessitate robust principles for accurate valuation and reporting.

This chapter offers a fundamental understanding of the Bitcoin blockchain's technical and economic intricacies, equipping auditors with the foundational knowledge to assess transaction reliability and address the unique challenges of auditing blockchain-based digital assets.

W. Olivier, P. Buys, *Auditing Bitcoin*,
https://doi.org/10.1007/978-981-95-5775-2_3

Keywords Auditing • Bitcoin • Blockchain technology • Cryptographic principles • Digital assets

JEL Classification M15 (IT Management): M42 (Auditing) • O31 (Innovation and Invention) • O33 (Technological Change)

3.1 Introduction

Building on the methodological justification of the BTC_AF development presented in the previous chapter, this chapter unpacks the basic blockchain architecture and principles of the Bitcoin blockchain, focusing on key audit considerations for assessing its associated bitcoin transactions and balances. It also examines the application of audit evidence within an assertion-based audit approach, as outlined in ISA 315 (Revised).

3.2 Decentralized Electronic Cash Systems

3.2.1 Background

Nakamoto's (2008) white paper outlines that Bitcoin is a decentralized electronic cash system that enables *peer-to-peer* (P2P) transactions without the need for intermediaries. According to Dzhereleiko et al. (2023), it functions as a transaction medium, with cryptocurrency exchanges facilitating global currency conversions.

At its core, the blockchain concept operates as a decentralized network where participants exchange digital currency units (e.g., bitcoin) via an open-source blockchain protocol, ensuring accessibility across diverse devices (Perez-Marco, 2016). Unlike physical currencies, bitcoin exists only digitally, with ownership asserted through cryptographic keys stored in digital wallets, granting users self-sovereignty over their assets (Puranam et al., 2019). Transactions are validated through the consensus mechanism referred to as *mining*, where participants solve cryptographic puzzles to maintain the blockchain's integrity. This decentralizes currency issuance and ensures deflationary dynamics by adhering to fixed protocol rules, which support a deflationary environment (Courtois & Bahack, 2014).

The blockchain serves as a public, immutable ledger for all transactions, governed by consensus rules and secured through the *proof-of-work* (PoW) algorithm, ensuring network integrity and resilience (Bouraga, 2021). The technology aspect addresses traditional payment system limitations by eliminating intermediaries, resisting censorship, overcoming cross-border transaction barriers, and enhancing security (Nabilou, 2020; Liu et al., 2018). As such, blockchain's cryptographic principles ensure security, transparency, and independence from centralized authorities.

3.2.2 *Transactional Process Flow*

Figure 3.1 illustrates the key components of the blockchain concept, including its principles and the process flow of digital coin transactions.

As illustrated, the transaction begins with User A transferring the bitcoin to User B by cryptographically signing it with the private keys. The transaction is forwarded to the mempool, which collates various pending transactions. Miners select transactions from the mempool to assemble a candidate block. During the mining process, miners compete to solve a complex cryptographic puzzle unique to that block. The first miner to solve the puzzle earns the right to add their block to the blockchain. Approximately every 10 minutes, a miner succeeds, integrating the block and its transactions into the blockchain. The new block, including User

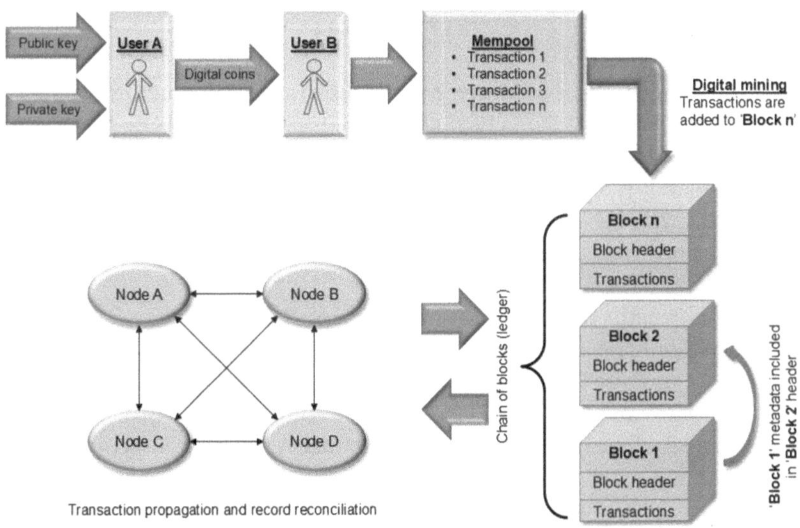

Fig. 3.1 Transaction process flow. (Adapted from Antonopoulos (2017); Dos Santos et al. (2019))

A's transaction, is verified by the network's nodes, which update the copies of the public ledger and share the update across the network. This distributed ledger technology ensures the blockchain's validity, accuracy, and completeness through mass reconciliation among nodes.

3.2.3 Blockchain Network Nodes

The network operates as a P2P system with a flat topology, where all nodes are equal and there is no central authority. The nodes serve three primary purposes, as follows:

- In maintaining the blockchain, the nodes store a complete copy of the blockchain, recording all transactions, enabling independent verification of transactions and blocks, and ensuring transparency and decentralization (Zhao et al., 2020).
- In relaying the data, the nodes propagate transactions and blocks across the network, keeping all participants updated and supporting the consensus mechanism (Decker & Wattenhofer, 2013).
- The mining nodes solve cryptographic puzzles by adding new blocks to the blockchain, earning rewards through newly minted bitcoin and transaction fees (Saad et al., 2021).

Furthermore, there are three basic types of nodes, including:

- Full nodes, the backbone of the network, store the entire blockchain, validate transactions, and ensure decentralization (Eisenbarth et al., 2021).
- Mining nodes are focused on block creation and rewards (Aljabr et al., 2019).
- Lightweight nodes rely on full nodes for transaction verification and store only necessary data (Antonopoulos, 2017).

Full nodes are particularly valuable for auditors as they provide a complete record of all transactions. This data can validate transaction occurrence, timing, and accuracy and determine *Unspent Transaction Output* (UTXO) balances, supporting assertions of existence, completeness, and valuation.

3.2.4 Mining in a Blockchain Ecosystem

As mentioned above, mining in the context of Bitcoin's ecosystem involves solving cryptographic puzzles using the SHA-256 hash function (Bertucci et al., 2020). Miners compete to find a *nonce*, a variable that produces a hash value below a target threshold, validating the block through the PoW (Grunspan & Pérez-Marco, 2020). This computationally intensive process ensures blockchain security and integrity, with the SHA-256 algorithm generating a unique 256-bit hash for each block (Courtois et al., 2014).

Miners expend computational resources and electricity to adjust the nonce until they meet the protocol's difficulty criteria, which are recalibrated periodically to ensure network stability (Fullmer & Morse, 2018). This resource intensity deters manipulation and supports decentralization. Furthermore, the miners are incentivized through block rewards, which consist of transaction fees and newly minted bitcoin distributed via a coinbase transaction.

Occasionally, simultaneous block discoveries create temporary blockchain forks, in which nodes temporarily follow different chains until the longest valid chain emerges, discarding orphaned blocks and returning their included transactions to the mempool for reprocessing (Neudecker & Hartenstein, 2019). Once six blocks are added after a transaction, it is considered highly secure and final (Kovalchuk et al., 2018), thus ensuring blockchain reliability, security, and decentralization.

3.2.5 Transactional Data

Participants construct and sign transactions using their public and private keys, which is then added to the mempool. Miners select it for inclusion in a candidate block until the block reaches capacity (Al-Shehabi, 2018). The transactions are then organized into a data structure called a Merkle Tree, and a hash of the data structure (the Merkle Root) is included in a block header. The block header contains metadata about the block, including the timestamp, previous block hash, and nonce (Puranam et al., 2019). Miners then hash the block header, competing to find a valid nonce for their candidate block. When a miner succeeds, the block is added to the blockchain, and the miner is rewarded through protocol incentives and transaction fees (Miller et al., 2015). Other miners and nodes verify the block to confirm the solution's validity. These transactions typically comprise the inputs (the funds spent), outputs (the funds received), transaction fees (the difference between inputs and outputs), and coinbase transactions (the newly minted bitcoin issued).

Coinbase transactions, the first in each block, have no inputs and generate bitcoin as a subsidy for miners through the PoW mechanism (Tasca et al., 2018). This is the only way new bitcoin are created, with outputs directed to miners' wallets as rewards (Saraswat et al., 2017). Other transactions in a block function as a double-entry accounting system, where inputs match outputs plus fees (Antonopoulos, 2017). Nakamoto (2008) explains that a Bitcoin block comprises transactional data, including the coinbase transaction and the block header, as shown in Figs. 3.2 and 3.3.

As illustrated above, the following are the components of a blockchain block:

- Block header: Metadata such as the block version, timestamp, and reference to the previous block hash, ensuring a chronological chain.
- Previous block hash: This link between the current block and its predecessor ensures blockchain integrity and immutability by invalidating subsequent blocks if altered.
- Version: Indicates the protocol version, enabling updates and improvements to the network.
- Merkle root: A hash of all transactions in the block, organized in a Merkle tree, ensuring transaction integrity and efficient verification.
- Nonce: A random value found during mining that generates a hash meeting the target threshold.
- Block size: Specifies the block's data capacity, influencing scalability and network throughput.
- Block height: Indicates the block's position in the chain, showing how many blocks precede it.
- Timestamp: Records when the block was mined according to the *Coordinated Universal Time* (UTC), aiding in chronological sequencing and providing auditors with insights for cut-off assertions.
- Difficulty target: The mining difficulty level is adjusted dynamically to maintain a consistent 10-minute block creation interval.

3.2.6 Wallets and Addresses

In blockchain technology, managing digital assets requires wallets and tools to safeguard private keys and facilitate transactions. A *wallet* can be

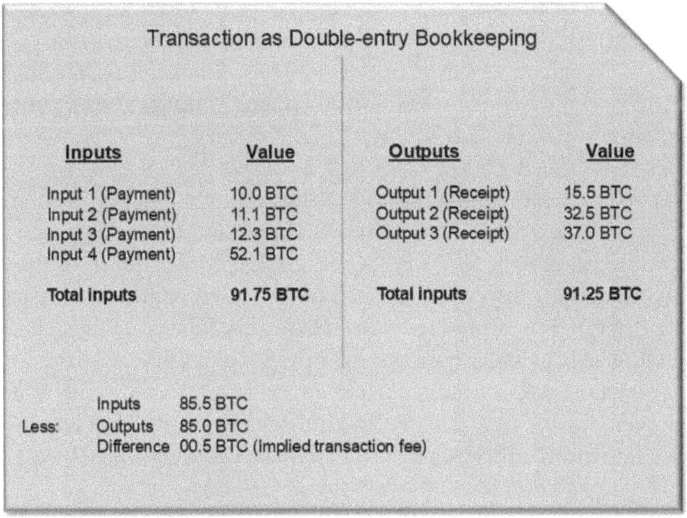

Fig. 3.2 Transaction as a double-entry booking

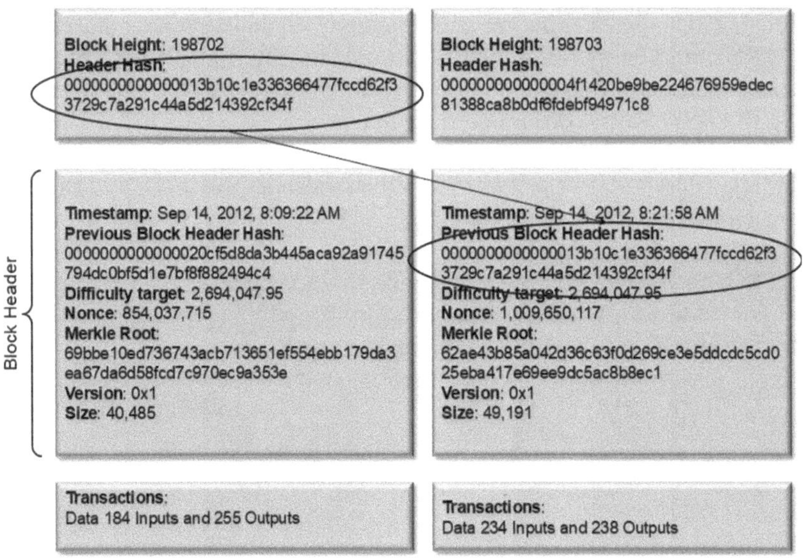

Fig. 3.3 Blockchain's block layout

either software or hardware for managing digital coins and storing private keys. In contrast, an *address* derived from the public key serves as a unique identifier for receiving funds (Liu et al., 2017). There are two wallet types, each with distinct features and security implications (Mirza & Rahulamathavan, 2023), as follows:

- Hot wallets are connected to the internet, enabling convenient, frequent transactions, but are more vulnerable to hacking and unauthorized access. Security breaches typically target the tools managing private keys, not the blockchain protocol. To mitigate risks, wallets are designed to minimize internet exposure (Gkaniatsou et al., 2017).
- Cold wallets, also known as cold storage, are offline, enhancing security against cyberattacks. While more secure, cold wallets are less convenient for frequent transactions and typically interact only with pre-approved addresses like hot wallets (Das et al., 2019).

3.2.7 Unspent Transaction Output

Unlike traditional accounting-based methods, the Bitcoin blockchain uses the UTXO model for transactions, in which each transaction generates new UTXOs representing unspent bitcoin (Delgado-Segura et al., 2019). UTXOs, tracked by full nodes, function like conventional currency, with values indicated by transaction outputs. Users spend UTXOs by referencing them as inputs, consuming their full value, and creating new UTXOs as outputs. A wallet's balance is the total value of all UTXOs linked to its address (Pérez-Solà et al., 2019). Wallets calculate balances by scanning the blockchain and consolidating spendable UTXOs controlled by the wallet's private key(s) (Wu & Wu, 2022). Each transaction consumes UTXOs and creates new ones, repeating this process across the blockchain.

For auditing purposes, the balance of an address can be verified by comparing the client's SoFP to the total unspent bitcoin at a specific block height and timestamp, ensuring the existence, valuation, and completeness of the reported assets.

3.3 Blockchain Network Scalability

3.3.1 Blockchain Trilemma

The blockchain trilemma highlights the challenge of optimizing decentralization, security, and scalability (Bayona Bultó, 2023). This trilemma, depicted in Fig. 3.4, highlights the trade-offs in balancing these aspects, asserting that it is impossible to maximize all three simultaneously (Werth et al., 2023).

In a blockchain context, decentralization ensures that no single entity has final control of the network (Park et al., 2019). Security protects the network from nefarious activities using cryptographic techniques and consensus mechanisms. At the same time, scalability refers to the network's capacity to efficiently handle growing transaction volumes without compromising performance or decentralization (Werth et al., 2023).

In layman's terms, with many globally distributed nodes, high decentralization can slow transactions and increase costs due to network congestion. Furthermore, enhanced security measures, like block validation mechanisms and hash rate increases, will hinder scalability by reducing efficiency. Balancing these aspects is a core challenge for developers, as improving one often compromises another (Garcia Saez, 2020). Blockchain protocols address these trade-offs through modifications such as hard or

Fig. 3.4 The blockchain trilemma

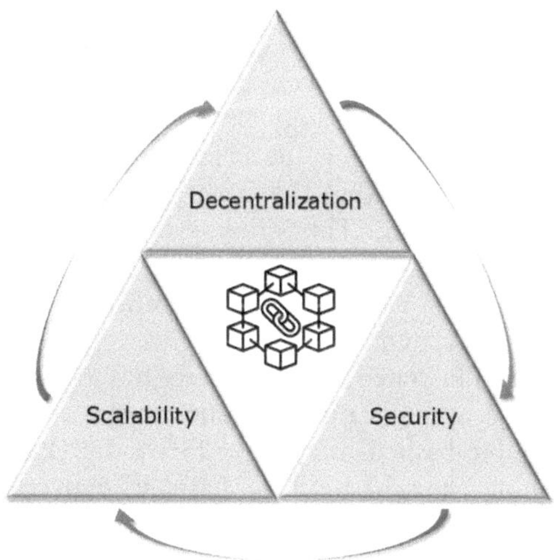

soft forks, creating side chains, or developing second-layer applications atop the layer-one blockchain, leveraging its core features.

3.3.2 Improvement Proposals

Improvement proposals are design documents proposing enhancements to the protocol. These documents are submitted by developers, researchers, and community members to address functionality, security, and scalability (Rubin, 2015) and facilitate structured discussions, reviews, and implementations of new features or improvements (Antonopoulos, 2017). They are categorized based on their compatibility with existing software:

- Soft forks are backward-compatible changes that introduce new rules or features. Older software can still recognize and validate blocks created under the new rules, maintaining a unified blockchain (De Almeida et al., 2019).
- Hard forks are incompatible changes requiring all participants to upgrade their software. Failure to do so can result in a permanent blockchain split, potentially creating a new cryptocurrency if there is community support (Thapa et al., 2021).

3.4 Access and Control Considerations

3.4.1 Public and Private Keys

As mentioned earlier, private and public key cryptography underpins blockchain technology. Private keys are randomly generated 256-bit numbers created using specialized hardware, software, or phrases processed through the SHA256 hash algorithm, which produces a deterministic 256-bit string. This string, typically represented as a 64-character hexadecimal sequence, functions as the private key (Singh & Singh, 2010). Figure 3.5 illustrates the generation of a public and private key pair and the associated address.

As illustrated, a 64-character hexadecimal private key undergoes elliptic curve multiplication to generate the corresponding public key, which is double-hashed using SHA256 and RIPEMD-160, producing a 160-bit public key hash. This hash is converted into an address through Base58Check encoding, which includes a version prefix and error-checking features to prevent entry errors by excluding visually similar characters like

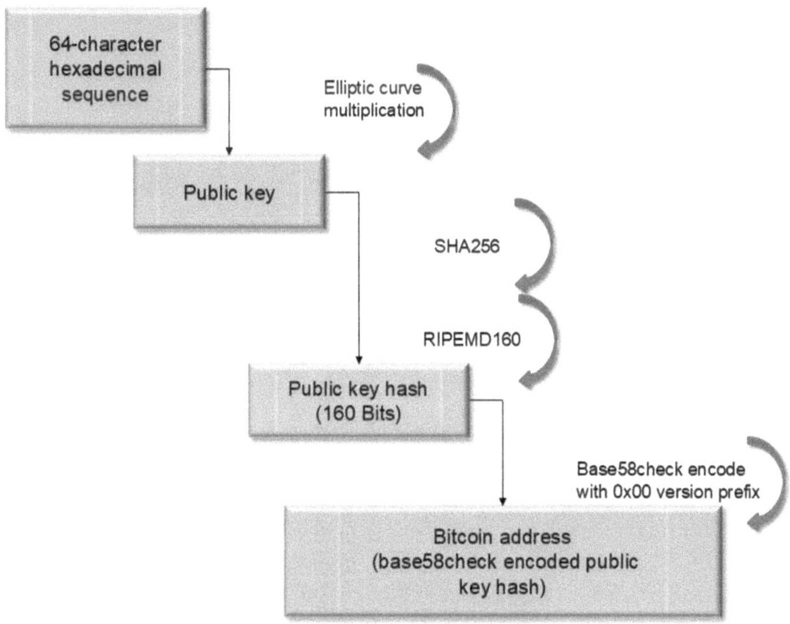

Fig. 3.5 Bitcoin address creation

I, O, l, 0, and 1 (Zhu et al., 2020). Base58Check version prefixes vary by address type:

- Mainnet addresses: Start with '1'.
- Wallet Import Format (WIF) private keys: Start with '5'.
- Extended public keys: Start with 'xpub'.
- Extended private keys: Start with 'xprv'.
- Multi-signature addresses: Start with '3'.
- SegWit (Bech32) addresses: Start with 'bc1' (mainnet).

These prefixes help users and applications efficiently manage the blockchain data and are introduced through soft forks. In the context of this book, the auditor may need to convert hexadecimal public key sequences into different address versions to verify ownership, illustrated in Table 3.1.

Table 3.1 shows how the hexadecimal public key can be converted into various blockchain address formats with distinct prefixes.

Table 3.1 Address version

Type	*Bitcoin address*	*Script*
PUBKEY	1SBYvnTz4fg9rV555cCSWnuQguvW14QR	OP_PUSHBYTES[33] 04423d14d34a2a6c5b 4057f133c4fda6fba3cf63edc2268e0e1e688041c6e1e6b9 OP_CHECKSIG
P2PKH	1SBYvnTz4fg9rV555cCSWnuQguvW14QR	OP_DUP OP_HASH160 OP_PUSHBYTES [20] 04c334c530707bfc078839866daf7f57e 5efbffe OP_EQUALVERIFY OP_CHECKSIG
P2SH_ P2WPKH	3QvCwWsKL4dRSmPN9KQtV5dbW2yPVVigRi	OP_HASH160 OP_PUSHBYTES[20] fec97 f320c0b027b16f582de0de6b1130873e817 OP _EQUAL
P2WPKH	Bc1qqnpnf3fhq7luq7yrnpnd4al40e09l0l78r4n87	OP_0 OP_PUSHBYTES[20] 04c334c53707bf c078839866daf7f57e5e5fbffe

3.4.2 *Cryptography Within the Blockchain*

Blockchain typically relies on two key cryptographic techniques, as follows:

- Digital signatures secure payment instructions and demonstrate control over an address, proving ownership of its assets - critical for auditor verification (Levitin, 2022).
- Cryptographic hash functions support functions like data storage, mining, and privacy (Badev & Chen, 2014), creating transaction IDs that act as unique fingerprints to summarize and locate transactions.

As shown in Fig. 3.6, a cryptographic signature created with the sender's public and private key(s) serves as proof of ownership and authorization for a transaction. When broadcast to the network, nodes use the public key and signature to confirm the transaction's authenticity, ensuring only the owner of the associated private key(s) authorized it (Hinkes, 2018). This process secures assets and facilitates safe transactions within the network.

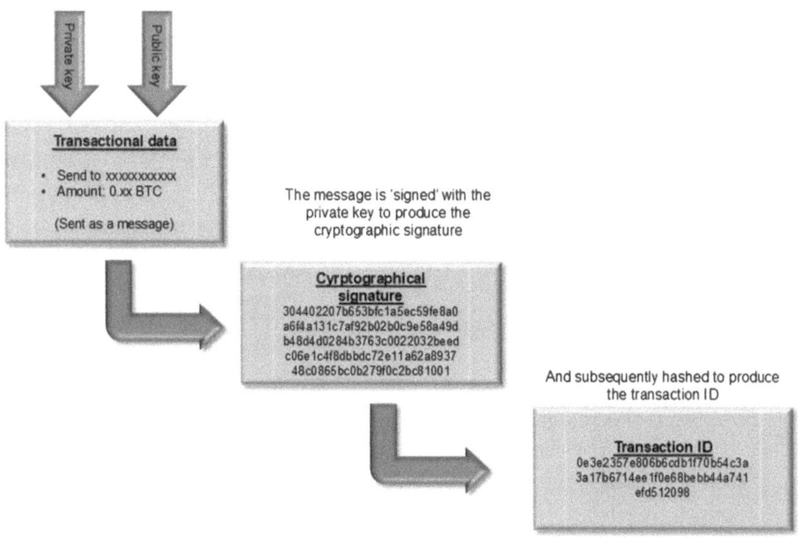

Fig. 3.6 Cryptographic message signature

In addition to signing transactional messages, cryptography enables the signing of non-transactional messages, allowing third parties to verify address control without exposing the private key(s) or impacting the blockchain (Rathore, 2020). Blockchain transactions function as cryptographically signed messages authorized by the private key corresponding to an address that holds the assets. Control of the private key is essential for authorizing transactions. Through asymmetric cryptography, participants validate transactions, ensuring their authenticity and integrity. This design enables auditors to verify public key control through message signing, thereby supporting cryptographic validation mechanisms.

3.4.3 Multi-Signature Addresses

Control of an address is determined by possession of the private key needed to sign valid transactions. Bitcoin Improvement Proposal 11 (BIP 11) introduced multi-signature addresses, enhancing security and transaction flexibility (Fabian et al., 2018). Unlike traditional addresses tied to a single private key, multi-signature addresses, also known as *Pay-to-Script Hash* (P2SH), require authorization from multiple private keys to complete a transaction (Antonopoulos, 2017).

As shown in Fig. 3.7, multi-signature addresses use an m-of-n signature setup, where 'm' is the threshold required for authorization, and 'n' is the total number of authorizing keys (Kara et al., 2023). This structure supports secure transaction types, such as escrow and joint accounts, preventing unilateral control by any single party (Yang et al., 2020).

Using elliptic curve cryptography, multi-signature addresses provide a robust framework for managing transactions (Zhang et al., 2022). When auditing multi-signature addresses, the auditor must evaluate three key aspects:

- Verify on the blockchain that the address is an m-of-n multi-signature address.
- Confirm that the required public key addresses (n) are correctly linked to the m-of-n multi-signature address.
- Ensure that the individuals controlling the (m) public key are the rightful owners of the associated private keys, using ownership verification methods.

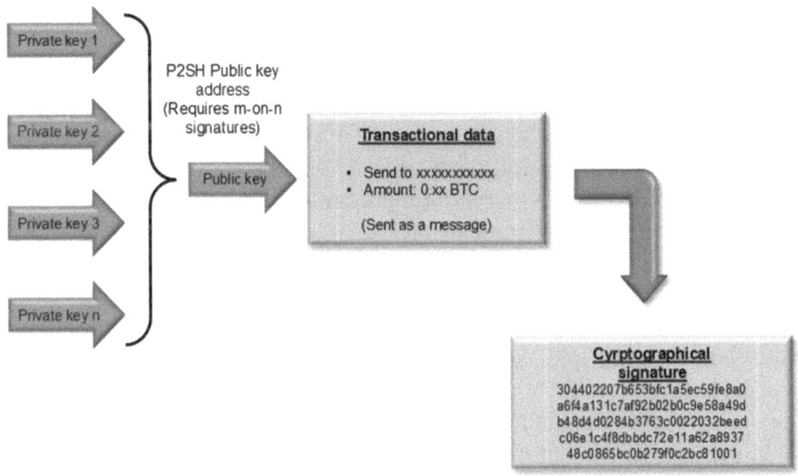

Fig. 3.7 Multi-signature address configuration

The 'P2SH Redeem Script' for an m-of-n multi-signature address
follows the pattern below:OP_PUSHNUM_2 OP_PUSHBYTES_33

<PublicKey1>
OP_PUSHBYTES_33
<PublicKey2>
OP_PUSHBYTES_33
<PublicKeyN>
OP_PUSHNUM_3 OP_CHECKMULTISIG

The <PublicKey1>, <PublicKey2>, and <PublicKeyN> keys, represented in hexadecimal format, must be converted into a specific address version before the cryptographic message signing.

3.4.4 *Extended Public Key (xpub) Addresses*

Hierarchical Deterministic (HD) wallets, defined by the BIP 32 standard, enable the generation of multiple child public keys from a single extended public key (xpub, ypub, or zpub) (Fornaro, 2017). These wallets, also known as seeded wallets, simplify key generation by deriving multiple keys from a single seed. HD wallets use a tree structure, allowing xpubs to generate sequences of child and grandchild keys to infinite depths (Rai et al., 2018), as shown in Fig. 3.8.

Derivation paths in HD wallets are sequences of indices that specify how child keys are derived from the master key. For example, in the format m/2/0, 'm' represents the master key, '2' indicates a hardened derivation, and '0' denotes the grandchild key index. Applying these paths to an xpub allows users to generate corresponding grandchild public keys (Gutoski & Stebila, 2015). A key advantage of HD wallets is their ability to derive public keys from parent public key(s) without requiring private key(s), enhancing security by enabling offline storage of private key(s). Private keys for different derivation levels are computed by sequentially modifying the seed (e.g., m/2/0) and applying the SHA256 hash function. This process ensures that each key is uniquely linked to the original seed, creating a secure, recoverable hierarchy of keys (Montes Valls, 2022).

Using the BIP32 standard, users can derive specific addresses by following the associated derivation path. The derived grandchild public key is converted into an address using hashing algorithms. This deterministic process links an xpub to multiple addresses. Auditors can use this approach to verify ownership of an xpub by connecting it to its child, grandchild,

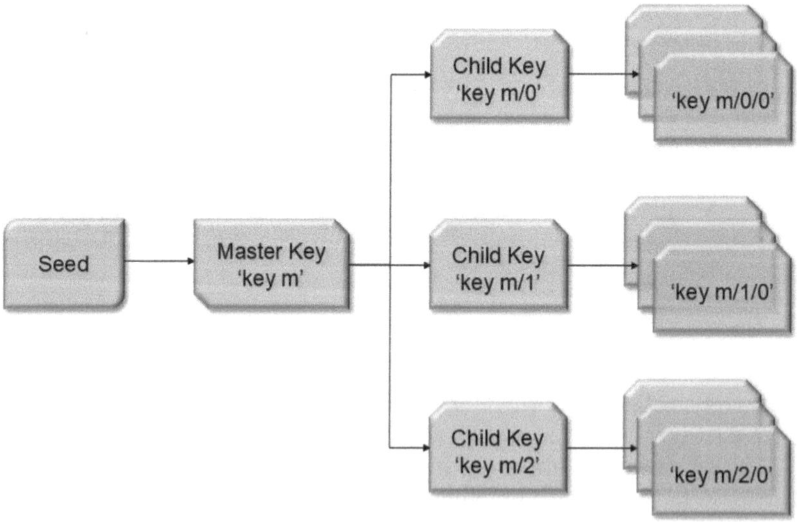

Fig. 3.8 Hierarchical deterministic wallets

and subsequent addresses via derivation paths. This effectively proves ownership of all linked addresses.

3.5 Market Dynamics

Bitcoin valuation is influenced by supply and demand dynamics across centralized exchanges, which lack a universal spot price (Ciaian et al., 2016). These exchanges match buy and sell orders, creating bid and ask prices that fluctuate with market conditions and participant sentiment (Barbon & Ranaldo, 2021). Unlike conventional assets, digital asset trading operates continuously, 24/7, across the globe, free from geographic or regulatory constraints (Feng et al., 2018).

As a result, the price of digital coins varies between exchanges and countries, often creating arbitrage opportunities due to differences in regulations and exchange controls. This decentralized structure supports a globally interconnected market, enabling traders to exploit price discrepancies and liquidity imbalances.

3.6 Summary

This chapter examined the Bitcoin blockchain's core elements, architecture, and market dynamics as a decentralized electronic cash system. It analyzes blockchain technology, covering transaction processing, architectural framework, mining, consensus mechanisms, and the trade-offs between scalability, security, and decentralization. This aims to equip auditors to understand relevant complexities and the technological foundations critical for verifying transaction data reliability. Additionally, exploring volatile market dynamics emphasizes auditing-related economic factors. These insights are essential for obtaining sufficient and appropriate audit evidence from blockchain records. The next chapter will focus on auditing principles that may serve as a foundation for the envisaged BTC_AF.

References

Aljabr, A. A., Sharma, A., & Kumar, K. (2019). Mining process in cryptocurrency using blockchain technology: Bitcoin as a case study. *Journal of Computational and Theoretical Nanoscience, 16*(10), 4293–4298.

Al-Shehabi, A. (2018). *Bitcoin transaction fee estimation using Mempool state and linear perceptron machine learning algorithm* (Master's project). San José State University. https://doi.org/10.31979/etd.j6zd-an2c

Antonopoulos, A. M. (2017). *Mastering bitcoin: Programming the open blockchain.* O'Reilly Media.

Badev, A. I., & Chen, M. (2014). *Bitcoin: Technical background and data analysis.* FEDS Working Paper, no. 2014-104. https://ssrn.com/abstract=2544331

Barbon, A., & Ranaldo, A. (2021). On the quality of cryptocurrency markets: Centralized versus decentralized exchanges. *arXiv preprint arXiv*, 2112.07386.

Bayona Bultó, Á. (2023). *A comprehensive evaluation of Ethereum, Solana, and Avalanche in addressing the blockchain trilemma* (Master's thesis). http://hdl.handle.net/11531/81462

Bertucci, C., Bertucci, L., Lasry, J. M., & Lions, P. L. (2020). Mean field game approach to bitcoin mining. *arXiv preprint arXiv*, 2004.08167.

Bouraga, S. (2021). A taxonomy of blockchain consensus protocols: A survey and classification framework. *Expert Systems with Applications, 168*, 114384.

Ciaian, P., Rajcaniova, M., & Kancs, D. A. (2016). The economics of bitcoin price formation. *Applied Economics, 48*(19), 1799–1815.

Courtois, N. T., & Bahack, L. (2014). On subversive miner strategies and block withholding attack in bitcoin digital currency. *arXiv preprint arXiv*, 1402.1718.

Courtois, N. T., Grajek, M., & Naik, R. (2014, September 22–24). Optimizing sha256 in bitcoin mining. In Z. Kotulski, B. Ksiezopolski, & K. Mazur (Eds.), *Cryptography and security systems: Third International Conference, CSS 2014, Lublin, Poland: Proceedings* (pp. 131–144). Springer.

Das, P., Faust, S., & Loss, J. (2019). A formal treatment of deterministic wallets. In *Proceedings of the 2019 ACM SIGSAC Conference on Computer and Communications Security.* https://doi.org/10.1145/3319535.3354236

De Almeida, T. L. G., Francois, P., & Frénot, S. (2019). *Forkmon: Monitoring the networks supporting bitcoin hard forks.* https://doi.org/10.1109/SRDSW49218.2019.00016

Decker, C., & Wattenhofer, R. (2013). Information propagation in the bitcoin network. In *IEEE P2P 2013 Proceedings.* https://doi.org/10.1109/P2P.2013.6688704

Delgado-Segura, S., Pérez-Sola, C., Navarro-Arribas, G., & Herrera-Joancomartí, J. (2019). Analysis of the bitcoin UTXO set. In A. Zohar, I. Eyal, V. Teague, J. Clark, A. Bracciali, F. Pintore, & M. Sala (Eds.), *Financial cryptography and data security* (pp. 78–91). Springer.

Dos Santos, S., Chukwuocha, C., Kamali, S., & Thulasiram, R. K. (2019, July). An efficient miner strategy for selecting cryptocurrency transactions. In *2019 IEEE International Conference on Blockchain (Blockchain)* (pp. 116–123). IEEE.

Dzhereleiko, S., Shevchenko, M. M., & Nazarova, T. Y. (2023). *Development of financial services based on cryptocurrencies.* https://repository.kpi.kharkov.ua/handle/KhPI-Press/71817

Eisenbarth, J. P., Cholez, T., & Perrin, O. (2021). A comprehensive study of the bitcoin p2p network. In *2021 3rd Conference on Blockchain Research & Applications for Innovative Networks and Services (BRAINS)* (pp. 105–112). https://ieeexplore.ieee.org/abstract/document/9569782

Fabian, B., Ermakova, T., Krah, J., Lando, E., & Ahrary, N. (2018). *Adoption of security and privacy measures in bitcoin–stated and actual behavior*. Available at SSRN https://ssrn.com/abstract=3184130

Feng, W., Wang, Y., & Zhang, Z. (2018). Informed trading in the bitcoin market. *Finance Research Letters, 26*, 63–70.

Fornaro, D. (2017). *Elliptic curve hierarchical deterministic private key sequences: Bitcoin standards and best practices* (Master's dissertation). https://www.politesi.polimi.it/handle/10589/140112

Fullmer, D., & Morse, A. S. (2018, December). Analysis of difficulty control in bitcoin and proof-of-work blockchains. In *2018 IEEE Conference on Decision and Control (CDC)* (pp. 5988–5992). IEEE.

Garcia Saez, M. I. (2020). Blockchain-enabled platforms: Challenges and recommendations. International *Journal of Interactive Multimedia and Artificial. Intelligence, 6*(3). https://doi.org/10.9781/ijimai.2020.08.005

Gkaniatsou, A., Arapinis, M., & Kiayias, A. (2017, November 22–24). Low-level attacks in bitcoin wallets. In Information Security: 20th International Conference, ISC 2017, Ho Chi Minh City, Vietnam. *Proceedings 20* (pp. 233–253). Springer International.

Grunspan, C., & Pérez-Marco, R. (2020). The mathematics of Bitcoin. *European Mathematical Society Magazine, 115*, 31–37.

Gutoski, G., & Stebila, D. (2015, January). Hierarchical deterministic bitcoin wallets that tolerate key leakage. In *International Conference on Financial Cryptography and Data Security* (pp. 497–504). Springer.

Hinkes, A. M. (2018). Throw away the key, or the key holder? Coercive contempt for lost or forgotten cryptocurrency private keys, or obstinate holders. *North-Western Journal of Technology and Intellectual Property, 16*(4), 225–263.

Kara, M., Laouid, A., & Hammoudeh, M. (2023). An efficient multi-signature scheme for blockchain. *Cryptology ePrint Archive.* https://eprint.iacr.org/2023/078

Kovalchuk, L., Kaidalov, D., Nastenko, A., Shevtsov, O., Rodinko, M., & Oliynykov, R. (2018, June). Number of confirmation blocks for bitcoin and ghost consensus protocols on networks with delayed message delivery. In *Proceedings of the 1st Workshop on Cryptocurrencies and Blockchains for Distributed Systems* (pp. 42–47). Association for Computing Machinery.

Levitin, A. J. (2022). Not your keys, not your coins: Unpriced credit risk in cryptocurrency. *Texas Law Review, 101*, 877–954.

Liu, Y., Li, R., Liu, X., Wang, J., Zhang, L., Tang, C., & Kang, H. (2017, October). An efficient method to enhance bitcoin wallet security. In *2017 11th IEEE International Conference on Anti-counterfeiting, Security, and Identification (ASID)* (pp. 26–29). IEEE. https://doi.org/10.1109/ICASID.2017.8285737

Liu, Y., Liu, X., Tang, C., Wang, J., & Zhang, L. (2018). Unlinkable coin mixing scheme for transaction privacy enhancement of bitcoin. *IEEE Access, 6*, 23261–23270. https://doi.org/10.1109/ACCESS.2018.2827163

Miller, A., Kosba, A., Katz, J., & Shi, E. (2015, October). Nonoutsourceable scratch-off puzzles to discourage bitcoin mining coalitions. In *Proceedings of the 22nd ACM Sigsac Conference on Computer and Communications Security* (pp. 680–691). https://doi.org/10.1145/2810103.2813621

Mirza, D., & Rahulamathavan, Y. (2023). Security analysis of android hot cryptocurrency wallet applications. In C. Hewage, Y. Rahulamathavan, & D. Ratnayake (Eds.), *Data protection in a post-pandemic society: Laws, regulations, best practices and recent solutions* (pp. 79–111). Springer.

Montes Valls, M. (2022). *Implementation of a secret sharing scheme in a Bitcoin wallet* (Bachelor thesis). http://hdl.handle.net/10459.1/83871

Nabilou, H. (2020). Bitcoin governance as a decentralized financial market infrastructure. *Stanford Journal of Blockchain Law & Policy, 4*(2), 177–202.

Nakamoto, S. (2008). *Bitcoin: A peer-to-peer electronic cash system.* https://assets.pubpub.org/d8wct41f/31611263538139.pdf

Neudecker, T., & Hartenstein, H. (2019, February 18–22). Short paper: An empirical analysis of blockchain forks in bitcoin. In Financial Cryptography and Data Security: 23rd International Conference, FC 2019, Frigate Bay, St. Kitts and Nevis. *Revised selected papers 23* (pp. 84–92). Springer International.

Park, S., Im, S., Seol, Y., & Paek, J. (2019). Nodes in the bitcoin network: Comparative measurement study and survey. *IEEE Access, 7*, 57009–57022.

Perez-Marco, R. (2016, June). Bitcoin and decentralized trust protocols. *The European Mathematical Society Newsletter*, 1–38. https://ems.press/content/serial-issue-files/13738#page=32

Pérez-Solà, C., Delgado-Segura, S., Navarro-Arribas, G., & Herrera-Joancomartí, J. (2019). Another coin bites the dust: An analysis of dust in UTXO-based cryptocurrencies. *Royal Society Open Science, 6*(1), 180817. https://doi.org/10.1098/rsos.180817

Puranam, K. S. R., Gaddam, M. C. T., Panda, S. K., & Reddy, G. (2019, February). Anatomy and lifecycle of a bitcoin transaction. In *Proceedings of International Conference on Sustainable Computing in Science, Technology and Management (SUSCOM), Amity University Rajasthan, Jaipur-India.* https://ssrn.com/abstract=3355106

Rai, D., Shetty, M. P., Alva, G. L., Hegde, A., & Shiran, M. (2018). Wallet for bitcoin cryptocurrency. *International Research Journal of Engineering and Technology, 5*(7), 2465–2467.

Rathore, P. S. (2020). Bitcoin: Mystery, history and background innovative technology involved. *International Journal for Research in Applied Science and Engineering Technology, 8*(3), 1010–1014.

Rubin, J. (2015). *Btcspark: Scalable analysis of the bitcoin blockchain using spark.* https://rubin.io/public/pdfs/s897report.pdf

Saad, M., Chen, S., & Mohaisen, D. (2021, November). Syncattack: Double-spending in bitcoin without mining power. In *Proceedings of the 2021 ACM SIGSAC Conference on Computer and Communications Security* (pp. 1668–1685). https://doi.org/10.1145/3460120.3484568

Saraswat, S., Chauhan, V. S., & Faujdar, N. (2017). Analysis on crypto-currency. *International Journal of Latest Trends in Engineering and Technology, 9*(1), 185–189.

Singh, D., & Singh, A. (2010). A secure private key encryption technique for data security in modern cryptosystem. *BIJIT-BVICAM's International Journal of Information Technology, 2*(2), 251–255.

Tasca, P., Hayes, A., & Liu, S. (2018). The evolution of the bitcoin economy: Extracting and analyzing the network of payment relationships. *The Journal of Risk Finance, 19*(2), 94–126.

Thapa, R., Sharma, P., Hüllmann, J. A., & Savarimuthu, B. T. R. (2021). Identifying influence mechanisms in permissionless blockchain communities: The bitcoin case. In *42nd International Conference on Information Systems (ICIS)* (pp. 1–17). https://www.joschka-huellmann.net/publications/2021-09-29-final-submission-icis.pdf

Werth, J., Berenjestanaki, M. H., Barzegar, H. R., El Ioini, N., & Pahl, C. (2023). A review of blockchain platforms based on the scalability, security and decentralization trilemma. *ICEIS, 1*, 146–155.

Wu, B., & Wu, B. (2022). *Blockchain for teens: With case studies and examples of blockchain across various industries*. Apress.

Yang, X., Lau, W. F., Ye, Q., Au, M. H., Liu, J. K., & Cheng, J. (2020). Practical escrow protocol for bitcoin. *IEEE Transactions on Information Forensics and Security, 15*, 3023–3034.

Zhang, H., Zou, X., Xie, G., & Li, Z. (2022, December 23–25). Blockchain multi-signature wallet system based on QR code communication. In Y. Sun, L. Cai, W. Wang, X. Song, & Z. Lu (Eds.), *Blockchain technology and application: 5th CCF China Blockchain Conference, CBCC 2022, Wuxi, China: Proceedings* (pp. 31–48). Springer Nature. https://doi.org/10.1007/978-981-19-8877-6_3

Zhao, Y., Niu, B., Li, P., & Fan, X. (2020, December 7–8). A novel enhanced lightweight node for blockchain. In Z. Zheng, H. N. Dai, M. Tang, & X. Chen (Eds.), *Blockchain and trustworthy systems: First International Conference, BlockSys 2019, Guangzhou, China, Proceedings 1* (pp. 137–149). Springer. https://doi.org/10.1007/978-981-15-2777-7_12

Zhu, L. H., Zheng, B. K., Shen, M., Gao, F., Li, H. Y., & Shi, K. X. (2020). Data security and privacy in bitcoin system: A survey. *Journal of Computer Science and Technology, 35*, 843–862.

CHAPTER 4

Audit Principles and Blockchain-Based Digital Assets

Abstract This chapter provides a comprehensive foundation for auditing bitcoin-associated balances and transactions. It sets the stage for developing the Bitcoin Audit Framework (BTC_AF) and examines the application of International Standards on Auditing (ISA) to blockchain-based digital assets. The chapter addresses the complexities auditors encounter in validating management assertions for entities engaging with these assets. Such practices range from self-custody to third-party custody. These practices have a significant impact on financial statement assertions related to transactions and balances. Using the *International Financial Reporting Standards* (IFRS) framework, the chapter outlines principles for recording blockchain-based digital assets in financial statements, ensuring transparency and compliance with relevant standards.

Key audit assertions, i.e., existence, ownership, completeness, valuation, and accuracy, are analyzed in the blockchain context. Challenges such as verifying multi-signature ownership and addressing valuation discrepancies across jurisdictions are also explored. In the context of bitcoin, substantive procedures are considered essential for addressing material transactions and balances while aligning audit practices with evolving regulatory and technological landscapes.

Keywords Auditing • Audit assertions • Bitcoin • Blockchain-based digital assets • Financial statements • Substantive procedures

W. Olivier, P. Buys, *Auditing Bitcoin*,
https://doi.org/10.1007/978-981-95-5775-2_4

JEL Classification M15 (IT Management): M42 (Auditing) • O31 (Innovation and Invention) • O33 (Technological Change)

4.1 Introduction

Building on the previous chapter's foundational overview of the Bitcoin blockchain's protocol, architecture, and related key considerations, this chapter examines auditing practices for blockchain-based digital assets. It explores the application of *International Standards on Auditing* (ISA) to entities holding such assets, outlining requisite audit procedures to obtain sufficient evidence for validating management assertions and addressing the interplay between traditional auditing standards and blockchain challenges.

4.2 Financial Reporting

4.2.1 Application of Digital Assets

The prior chapters established the dual nature of blockchain-based digital assets as *peer-to-peer* (P2P) digital currencies and speculative assets. As acknowledged earlier, its economic attributes support its use as currency, fulfilling the roles of a medium of exchange and store of value. In this context, business entities must record such transactions in their accounting ledgers.

Entities engaging with blockchain-based digital assets typically fall into three categories: transactional users, custodians, and investors, which can be classified as a *Virtual Asset Service Provider* (VASP) or non-VASP. VASPs, typically including trading platforms, wallet providers, and custodians, facilitate blockchain-based digital asset transactions. In contrast, non-VASPs use such assets as a store of value, for speculative purposes, as a hedge against fiat currency devaluation, or as a payment method when accepted by suppliers.

4.2.2 Custody of Digital Assets

Entities engaging with blockchain-based digital assets must decide between self-custody and third-party custody for asset management:

- Self-custody involves the user managing private key(s) linked to their wallet and blockchain-based digital assets (Antonopoulos, 2017). This approach appeals to those seeking complete control to avoid reliance on third-party transparency and security. However, it does expose risks such as theft, breaches, or device failure, highlighting the importance of secure key management (Au et al., 2020).
- Third-party custody entrusts private key management to external entities, like cryptocurrency exchanges or custodial service providers (Kokorin et al., 2020). These entities ensure secure storage and provide access via standard authentication methods.

Understanding custody practices, whether by VASPs or non-VASPs, is crucial for evaluating the impact of transactions on the blockchain and accounting records (Di Nicola et al., 2020). Figure 4.1 illustrates conceptual self-custody transaction scenarios, which will shape how auditors gather evidence, as explored later in the chapter.

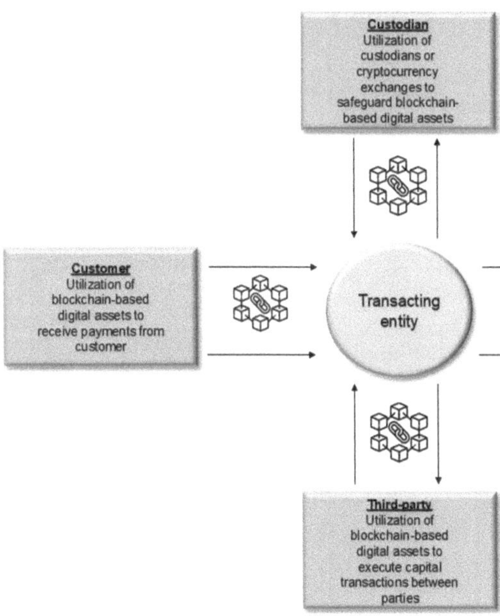

Fig. 4.1 Conceptual transactional flow

As illustrated, there is a vertical flow of blockchain-based digital assets in capital transactions and a horizontal flow in transactional payments and receipts. Hybrid custodians, such as cryptocurrency exchanges, facilitate transactions, such as buying and selling assets, for fees that are compensated in digital assets or fiat currency, depending on the transaction type (Barbon & Ranaldo, 2021). These transactions occur off-chain, directly affecting the custodian's back-end systems rather than the blockchain, with funds transferred between customer and corporate accounts.

Off-chain transactions, commonly used by brokers to reduce fees, can result in the commingling of funds under specific regulations or operational setups. The implications differ based on whether the asset operates on an account-based system (e.g., Ethereum), a *Unspent Transaction Output* (UTXO)-based system (e.g., Bitcoin) (Zahnentferner, 2018), or whether the blockchain has smart contract functionality.

This principle applies to transactions between two parties using a mutual custodian's ERP system. Figure 4.2 depicts these flows and their impact on the blockchain or the custodian's back-end records.

Figure 4.2 depicts the various transactional flows of blockchain-based digital assets, including buying, selling, sending, and receiving bitcoin

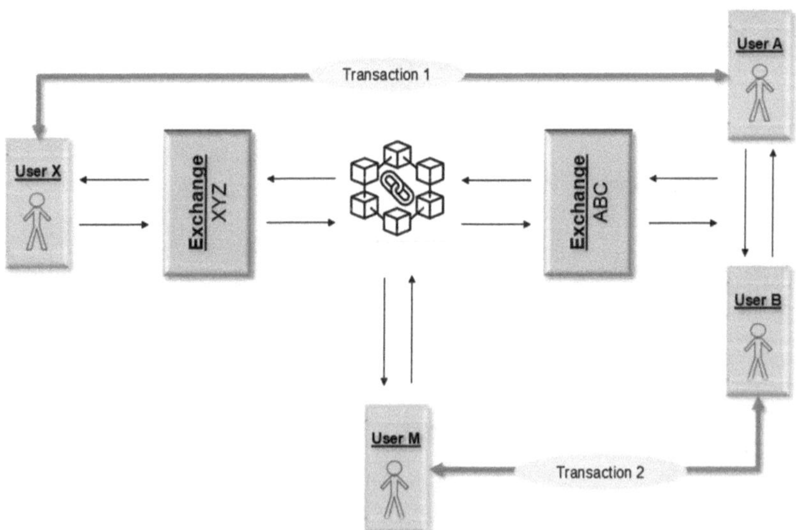

Fig. 4.2 P2P transactional flow

within an exchange, and whether or not these are recorded on the blockchain. According to the illustration, in *Transaction 1*, where User A sends and receives bitcoin from User X, User A uses Exchange ABC, while User X uses Exchange XYZ. In the case of *Transaction 2* between User B and User M, User B would also use Exchange ABC, while User M would apply self-custody. Furthermore, transactions between users on the same custodian, e.g., User A and User B, have no impact on the blockchain.

4.2.3 *Financial Statement Impact*

Legislation worldwide, including South Africa's Companies Act (2008), the US Internal Revenue Code (1986), and the UK Companies Act (2006), requires businesses to maintain accounting records for all transactions in compliance with accepted accounting frameworks. The BTC_AF adopts the *International Financial Reporting Standards* (IFRS) framework for blockchain-based digital assets.

The IFRS Conceptual Framework for Financial Reporting provides principles guiding global accounting standards, ensuring consistency and aiding decision-making for preparers, users, and standard-setters (Kabir & Rahman, 2018). It outlines key financial statement elements, such as assets, income, and expenses, summarized in Table 4.1.

The IFRS Interpretations Committee determined that blockchain-based digital assets qualify as assets (Pelucio-Grecco et al., 2020). When used as a medium of exchange, it also meets the definitions of income and expense. Thus, blockchain-based digital asset balances should be recorded in the *Statement of Financial Position* (SoFP), and related transactions should appear in the *Statement of Profit and Loss* (SoPL). This ensures

Table 4.1 Financial statement elements

Element	*Description*
Asset	A right that can generate economic benefits is defined as a current economic resource controlled by an entity due to past events.
Income	Increases in assets or decreases in liabilities that raise equity, excluding contributions from equity holders.
Expense	Decreases in assets or increases in liabilities that reduce equity, excluding distributions to equity holders.

Adapted from IFRS (2023)

transparency, consistency, and accuracy in reporting, providing stakeholders with essential insights into the asset's management and use.

4.2.4 *Statutory and Regulatory Requirements*

As noted earlier, entities dealing with blockchain-based digital assets may be required by law or regulation to have their financial statements audited by an independent third-party auditor under the ISA or similar auditing frameworks. As defined by the ISA, the auditor's primary role is to ensure that the financial statements are free of material misstatements, whether caused by fraud or error (Velentzas et al., 2017). This involves evaluating accounting policies, estimates, and related disclosures for compliance with the applicable accounting framework.

4.3 Financial Audit

4.3.1 *Evolution of the Financial Audit Function*

Auditing dates back to ancient civilizations, including Rome, Greece, China, and Egypt, where clerks verified merchants' goods, originating from the Latin word audire (meaning "to hear" or "to listen"). In 1494, Luca Pacioli published the first book on double-entry accounting, a cornerstone of modern accounting, and advocated independent third-party verification to prevent fraud (Smith, 2018). Over time, auditing has evolved from primarily focusing on fraud detection to also enhancing the credibility of financial reporting and fostering stakeholder trust. Ajao et al. (2016) assert that auditing is a systematic and impartial review of financial records to confirm their alignment with recognized criteria, with findings conveyed through an audit opinion.

Today, many regulatory accounting bodies follow the protocols of the *International Federation of Accountants* (IFAC), ensuring high auditor independence and integrity through guidelines such as the *International Standards on Assurance Engagements* (ISAEs) (Church et al., 2015). According to ISA 700, the auditor aims to evaluate evidence and express an 'audit opinion' on financial statements in a written report, which influences stakeholders' decisions and ensures corporate accountability and transparency (Tian & Xin, 2017). The audit opinion, therefore, verifies the accuracy and reliability of financial information, emphasizing the critical role of sufficient and appropriate evidence.

4.3.2 Audit Process

The audit process consists of four stages, each involving specific tasks and corresponding audit standards, outlined in Table 4.2.

Table 4.2 outlines the four stages of the audit process along with their respective tasks and relevant ISA standards. The envisaged BTC_AF is intended to guide auditors in performing substantive procedures to obtain evidence for entities engaging with bitcoin, whether these assets are held on the SoFP or used in transactions reflected in the SoPL.

ISA 700 specifies two objectives: forming an opinion on financial statements based on evaluated evidence and clearly expressing this opinion in a written report (IAASB, 2022). As Meleschenko et al. (2020) emphasize, obtaining audit evidence is central to auditing, achieved through substantive procedures or a combination of substantive procedures and tests of controls.

ISA 330 differentiates these approaches: substantive procedures test transactions, balances, and accounts for material misstatements, while tests of controls assess the effectiveness of controls in preventing or detecting such misstatements (Leonov et al., 2018). According to ISA 330, auditors may adopt a purely substantive approach when controls are ineffective or when substantive procedures are more efficient for addressing risks (IAASB, 2022). However, substantive procedures are always required for material transactions, balances, and disclosures, even if controls are tested (DeBoer et al., 2014).

Take note that since the BTC_AF will prioritize a *substantive* audit approach, *tests of controls* will not be considered.

4.4 Assertion-Based Audit Approach

4.4.1 ISA 500: Audit Evidence

At the heart of auditing is the collection and analysis of evidence to support or refute management's financial assertions (Barr-Pulliam et al., 2024). ISA 500 defines audit evidence as "the information used by the auditor in arriving at the conclusions on which the auditor's opinion is based" (IAASB, 2022). Auditors must design procedures to obtain sufficient and relevant evidence, ensuring alignment with the specific assertions being tested.

Table 4.2 Applicable audit standards

Stage	*Task*	*Standard*
Planning	Client acceptance and continuance	**ISA 200**: Overall objectives of the independent auditor and the conduct of an audit following the *International Standards on Auditing* **ISA 220**: Quality control for an audit of financial statements **ISA 300**: Planning and audit of financial statements **ISA 402**: Audit considerations relating to an entity using a service organization
	Understanding the client	**ISA 300**: Planning and audit of financial statements **ISA 402**: Audit considerations relating to an entity using a service organization
Risk assessment		**ISA 300**: Planning and audit of financial statements **ISA 315 (Revised)**: Identifying and assessing the risks of material misstatement **ISA 320**: Materiality in planning and performing an audit **ISA 330**: The auditor's responses to assessed risks **ISA 402**: Audit considerations relating to an entity using a service organization
Evidence gathering	Internal control assessment	**ISA 265**: Communicating deficiencies in internal controls to those charged with governance and management
	Test of internal controls	**ISA 500**: Audit evidence **ISA 501**: Audit evidence – Specific considerations for selected items
	Substantive procedures	**ISA 500**: Audit evidence **ISA 505**: External confirmations **ISA 520**: Analytical procedures **ISA 540**: Auditing accounting estimates, including Fair Value Accounting estimates and related disclosures **ISA 550**: Related parties Audit evidence – Specific considerations for selected items
Completion	Overview of the financial report	**ISA 560**: Subsequent events

(*continued*)

Table 4.2 (continued)

Stage	*Task*	*Standard*
	Audit report	**ISA 700**: Forming an opinion and reporting on financial statements **ISA 706**: Emphasis of *Matter Paragraphs* and *Other Matter Paragraphs* in the independent auditor's report.

Adapted from IAASB (2022)

Advances in technology have transformed how (audit) evidence is gathered and analyzed (Barr-Pulliam et al., 2022). These innovations and the complexities of globalized and digitized operations have heightened the challenges of addressing material misstatement risks (Liu & Lai, 2012). In this context, auditors must adapt to diverse standards and technologies, requiring specialized skills to effectively gather valid evidence from digital sources (Brown-Liburd et al., 2015).

The reliability of evidence depends on its source, with independent and objective sources, such as bank statements or third-party confirmations, deemed most trustworthy (Johari et al., 2022). Evidence independently obtained by the auditor, such as blockchain-related data, is similarly robust (Barr-Pulliam et al., 2024), underscoring its value in modern auditing.

4.4.2 *Audit Assertions*

Sherstiuk (2022) explains that auditors evaluate management's financial statement assertions, including completeness, rights and obligations, valuation, and existence (SoFP), as well as the completeness, occurrence, cut-off, and accuracy of transactions (SoPL), and the presentation and disclosure of balances and transactions (IAASB, 2022). These assertions are not accepted at face value; auditors must gather corroborative evidence to verify their accuracy, forming the basis of the audit opinion and ensuring the integrity of the financial audit process.

Lessambo (2018) emphasizes the central role of assertions in financial audits, with auditors primarily using substantive procedures to validate them. Fukukawa and Mock (2012) highlight the iterative nature of assessing risks tied to assertions, a perspective supported by Barr-Pulliam et al. (2024), who emphasize that audit evidence either validates or refutes management's claims. It is therefore accepted that assessing assertions requires auditors to evaluate the risk of material misstatement at the assertion level and design audit procedures to address these risks.

4.4.3 *ISA 315 (Revised) and Audit Assertions*

ISA 315 (Revised) aims to help auditors identify and assess the risk of material misstatement, whether due to fraud or error, at both the financial statement and assertion levels (IAASB, 2022). Szívós and Orosz (2014) highlight the inherent risk in auditing financial statements, where individual or aggregated misstatements can bypass detection, prevention, or correction by internal controls.

Paragraph 12(a) of ISA 315 (Revised) defines assertions as management's explicit or implicit representations about the recognition, measurement, presentation, and disclosure of financial information based on the applicable reporting framework. Assertions guide auditors in identifying, assessing, and addressing potential misstatements.

Tables 4.3 and 4.4 summarize and compare applicable management assertions, the corresponding audit evidence, and objectives for verifying or disputing these assertions.

Deng and Peng (2022) emphasize that auditing relies on evaluating management's assertions, requiring auditors to meticulously gather

Table 4.3 Audit assertions and audit objectives

Assertation	*Objective*
Occurrence	Determine whether recorded or disclosed transactions and events have occurred and pertain to the entity.
Completeness	Ensure all required transactions, events, and related disclosures are accurately recorded and included in the financial statements.
Accuracy	Ensure that recorded transaction amounts, data, and related disclosures are accurate, properly measured, and accurately described.
Cut-off	Ensure transactions and events are recorded in the correct accounting period.
Classification	Ensure transactions and events are accurately recorded in the correct accounts.
Presentation and disclosure	Transactions and events are properly aggregated or disaggregated, clearly described, and accompanied by relevant disclosures in accordance with the applicable financial reporting framework.

Adapted from IAASB (2022), AICPA (2021), and ACCA (2015)

Table 4.4 Financial statement assertions and audit objectives

Assertation	*Objective*
Existence	Confirm the existence of assets, liabilities, and equity interests.
Rights and obligations	Confirm the entity's control over assets and its obligations in terms of related liabilities.
Completeness	All assets, liabilities, equity interests, and related disclosures have been properly recorded and included in the financial statements.
Valuation, accuracy, and allocation	To ensure assets, liabilities, and equity interests are recorded at appropriate amounts, with valuation or allocation adjustments and related disclosures accurately measured and described.
Classification	Assets, liabilities, and equity interests are recorded in the correct accounts.
Presentation and disclosure	Assets, liabilities, and equity interests are properly aggregated or disaggregated, clearly described, and accompanied by relevant and understandable disclosures under the financial reporting framework.

Adapted from IAASB (2022), AICPA (2021), and ACCA (2015)

evidence to verify these claims and assess material misstatement risks at the assertion level.

4.4.4 *Audit Programs*

Audit programs are essential in audit engagements, guiding auditors to gather sufficient evidence to support assertions and substantiate the audit opinion (Hammersley and Ricci, 2021). These programs are tailored to each *Financial Statement Area* (FSA) since procedures and relevant assertions vary across FSAs.

Luo and Yu (2022) opine that, for blockchain-based digital asset purposes, audit programs must be designed to address both their inclusion in the SoFP and their use in transactions affecting the SoPL. The BTC_AF will include specific audit programs for the SoFP and SoPL, as outlined in Table 4.5. This table summarizes the assertions and procedures required to gather reliable evidence, highlighting the diverse approaches auditors must take to ensure the accuracy and integrity of blockchain-based digital asset transactions and balances.

Table 4.5 Key assertions and audit considerations

Assertion	*Consideration*
Existence	Verify whether the asset exists physically or digitally by conducting appropriate verification procedures.
Rights and obligations	Confirm the entity's ownership or control of the asset by reviewing documentation validating its rights or obligations.
Completeness	Ensure all transactions are recorded by reviewing accounting records for completeness.
Accuracy and valuation	Inspect details, currency amounts, and account allocations to verify that transactions and balances are accurate and properly valued.
Cut-off	Ensure transactions are recorded in the correct period by assessing their timing, especially near the period ends.
Occurrence	Confirm transactions occurred by corroborating them with third-party evidence, such as bank statements.
Classification	Ensure all required disclosures are complete and accurate by reviewing the financial statements.

Adapted from Vincent and Wilkins (2020); Marx et al. (2021)

4.4.5 *Audit Assertions in Blockchain Context*

Assertions regarding account balances and transactions address the various FSAs featured in the SoFP and SoPL. Accordingly, auditors must gather adequate and relevant audit evidence to substantiate these assertions when evaluating account balances in the SoFP and transactions in the SoPL that involve blockchain-based digital assets, which can be defined as follows:

- Existence: Auditors must verify whether assets exist physically or digitally. For blockchain-based digital assets, existence is determined via the blockchain, a public ledger. Auditors can independently confirm transactions and balances linked to specific addresses using a full node. The decentralized and immutable nature of blockchain ensures definitive evidence of existence at a particular timestamp.
- Rights and obligations: Auditors assess whether an entity has control over its blockchain-based digital assets. Ownership is tied to possessing the private key(s) of an address. Multi-signature (m-of-n) setups or extended public keys (xpubs) require auditors to validate control over all relevant keys. Auditors may request that address owners sign a unique phrase or execute a blockchain transaction to confirm ownership.

- Completeness: Auditors ensure all balances are accounted for by comparing client-provided data with internal and external sources, such as a reconciled full node. This process verifies that all relevant transactions and addresses are included.
- Presentation and disclosure: Auditors evaluate whether financial statement disclosures align with applicable standards. Blockchain-based digital assets held for sale are governed by IAS 2 (Inventories), while other holdings fall under IAS 38 (Intangible Assets). Auditors must confirm that appropriate classification and valuation methods are used under IFRS.
- Valuation: Blockchain-based digital assets must be accurately valued at reporting dates. Auditors reference market values to determine the digital assets' fiat currency equivalent, accounting for jurisdictional differences, arbitrage, and exchange rates. Consistency with the entity's accounting policy on timestamps is essential.
- Occurrence: Auditors verify that transactions occurred by confirming their inclusion in the blockchain. Block finality is typically assured after six subsequent blocks, ensuring minimal risk of reversal.
- Completeness: Auditors trace transactions from the blockchain to accounting records, ensuring all transactions have been recorded accurately.
- Cut-off: Transactions are checked to ensure they are recorded in the correct financial period. Blockchain timestamps provide reliable evidence for determining the appropriate period.
- Accuracy: Transactions must be recorded precisely in the accounting records. Auditors validate notional and fiat values using blockchain data and independent pricing sources, taking into account jurisdictional factors.
- Classification: Classification assertions align closely with presentation and disclosure, ensuring transactions are appropriately categorized within financial statements.

The BTC_AF integrates these assertions into audit programs tailored to blockchain-based digital assets, emphasizing the use of blockchain's inherent transparency and immutability to support robust audit evidence. The above assertions will form the *audit basis* for the BTC_AF development.

4.5 Summary

This chapter examined audit principles for entities with blockchain-based digital assets, with a focus on applying traditional auditing standards to both VASPs and non-VASPs. It highlighted critical audit procedures, challenges, and considerations for obtaining sufficient evidence and addressed the unique complexities of auditing assertions related to this asset class. It explored financial reporting for blockchain-based digital assets, including their application, custody, and impact on financial statements, and emphasized compliance with statutory and regulatory requirements and the evolving landscape of audit practices.

An assertion-based audit approach is highlighted, with ISA 500 and ISA 315 (Revised) guiding the evaluation of audit evidence and assertions. Applying these assertions to the blockchain is detailed, covering key areas such as existence, ownership, completeness, valuation, and accuracy of account balances and transactions. The next chapter will focus on the first design iteration, i.e., the problem-centric iteration, in which the 1st Expert Team will be engaged.

References

Ajao, O. S., Olamide, J. O., & Temitope, A. A. (2016). Evolution and development of auditing. *Unique Journal of Business Management Research, 3*(1), 32–40.

American Institute of Certified Public Accountants. (2021). Codification of statements on auditing standards: AU-C section 315 – Understanding the entity and its environment and assessing the risks of material misstatement. In *AICPA professional standards* (Vol. 1). AICPA.

Antonopoulos, A. M. (2017). *Mastering bitcoin: Programming the open blockchain.* O'Reilly Media.

Association of Certified Chartered Accountants (UK). (2015). *Audit and assurance: Specific considerations.* https://www.accaglobal.com/africa/en/member/discover/cpd-articles/audit-assurance/specific-considerations.html

Au, A., Hoffman, M., Mattingly, J., McAteer, P., & Takahashi, Y. (2020). *Care, custody, & control (CCC): Identification, quantification, and mitigation of cryptocurrency custodial risk.* https://www.paulmcateer.com/wp-content/uploads/2021/01/CCC_Pub_Version.pdf

Barbon, A., & Ranaldo, A. (2021). On the quality of cryptocurrency markets: Centralized versus decentralized exchanges. *arXiv preprint arXiv*, 2112.07386.

Barr-Pulliam, D., Brown-Liburd, H. L., & Munoko, I. (2022). The effects of person-specific, task, and environmental factors on digital transformation and innovation in auditing: A review of the literature. *Journal of International Financial Management & Accounting, 33*, 337–374.

Barr-Pulliam, D., Calvin, C. G., Eulerich, M., & Maghakyan, A. (2024). Audit evidence, technology, and judgement: A review of the literature in response to ED-500. *Journal of International Financial Management & Accounting, 35*(1), 36–67.

Brown-Liburd, H., Issa, H., & Lombardi, D. (2015). Behavioral implications of big data's impact on audit judgment and decision making and future research directions. *Accounting Horizons, 29*(2), 451–468.

Church, B. K., Jenkins, J. G., McCracken, S. A., Roush, P. B., & Stanley, J. D. (2015). Auditor independence in fact: Research, regulatory, and practice implications drawn from experimental and archival research. *Accounting Horizons, 29*(1), 217–238.

DeBoer, M., Eimers, P., & Elsas, P. (2014, June 2014). *Reengineering the audit in a digitized environment: Developments in practice, challenges for auditing standards and opportunities for further research.* Paper submitted to the 20th Annual International Symposium on Audit Research. https://www.isarhq.org/2014_downloads/papers/ISAR2014_Boer_Eimers_Elsas.pdf

Deng, L., & Peng, J. (2022). Reflections on the concept, classification and application of assertion under the new standards. *Frontiers in Business, Economics and Management, 5*(3), 64–68.

Di Nicola, V., Longo, R., Mazzone, F., & Russo, G. (2020). Resilient custody of crypto-assets, and threshold multisignatures. *Mathematics, 8*(10), 1773. https://doi.org/10.3390/math8101773

Fukukawa, H., & Mock, T. J. (2012). Auditors' evidence evaluation and aggregation using beliefs and probabilities. *International Journal of Approximate Reasoning, 53*(2), 190–199.

Hammersley, J. S., & Ricci, M. A. (2021). Using audit programs to improve auditor evidence collection. *The Accounting Review, 96*(1), 251–272.

IFRS. (2023). IFRS. Ifrs.org. https://www.ifrs.org/

International Auditing and Assurance Standards Board. (2022). *Handbook of international quality management, auditing, review, other assurance, and related services pronouncements.* International Federation of Accountants.

Johari, R., Mohd Hati, T., & Hussin, S. (2022). Factors influencing auditors' professional scepticism: Malaysian evidence. *Universal Journal of Accounting and Finance, 10*(1), 243–253.

Kabir, H., & Rahman, A. (2018). How does the IASB use the conceptual framework in developing IFRSs? An examination of the development of IFRS 16 leases. *Journal of Financial Reporting, 3*(1), 93–116.

Kokorin, I., De Graaf, T., & Haentjens, M. (2020). The failed hopes of disintermediation: Crypto-custodian insolvency, legal risks and how to avoid them. *Singapore Journal of Legal Studies, 2020*, 526–563.

Leonov, P. Y., Leonova, E. K., Veselova, E. A., & Kotelyanets, O. S. (2018). General scheme of risk–oriented audit stages. *KnE Engineering*, 402–415. https://doi.org/10.18502/keg.v3i6.3021

Lessambo, F. I. (2018). *Financial statements: Analysis and reporting*. Palgrave Macmillan.

Liu, C. L., & Lai, S. M. (2012). Organizational complexity and auditor quality. *Corporate Governance: An International Review, 20*(4), 352–368.

Luo, M., & Yu, S. (2022). Financial reporting for cryptocurrency. *Review of Accounting Studies, 29*(2), 1707–1740.

Marx, B., Bourne, M., Hamel, A., & Van der Watt, E. (2021). *Dynamic auditing* (14th ed.). LexisNexis South Africa.

Meleschenko, S. S., Snetkova, T. A., Lyzhova, A. V., Markaryan, S. E., & Khafizova, L. V. (2020). Aspects of environmental issues in the audit evidence. *Procedia Environmental Science, Engineering and Management, 7*(3), 395–407.

Pelucio-Grecco, M. C., Santos Neto, J. P. D., & Constancio, D. (2020). Accounting for bitcoins in light of IFRS and tax aspects. *Revista Contabilidade & Finanças, 31*, 275–283.

Sherstiuk, O. (2022). Audit methods for financial assets information disclosure. *Oblik i finansi, 1*, 141–147.

Smith, M. (2018). *Luca Pacioli: The father of accounting*. Available at SSRN https://ssrn.com/abstract=2320658

Szívós, L., & Orosz, I. (2014). The role of data authentication and security in the audit of financial statements. *Acta Polytechnica Hungarica, 11*(8), 161–176.

Tian, J., & Xin, M. (2017). Literature review on audit opinion. *Journal of Modern Accounting and Auditing, 13*(6), 266–271.

Velentzas, J., Broni, G., & Kartalis, N. (2017). Deterrence, detection, and investigation of economic fraud and auditor's responsibilities relating to audit of financial statements according to international standards. In N. Tsounis, & A. Vlachvei (Eds.), *Advances in applied economic research: Proceedings of the 2016 International Conference on Applied Economics (ICOAE)* (pp. 719–742). Springer. https://doi.org/10.1007/978-3-319-48454-9_49

Vincent, N. E., & Wilkins, A. M. (2020). Challenges when auditing cryptocurrencies. *Current Issues in Auditing, 14*(1), A46–A58.

Zahnentferner, J. (2018). Chimeric ledgers: Translating and unifying utxo-based and account-based cryptocurrencies. Cryptology ePrint Archive, paper 2018/262. https://ia.cr/2018/262

CHAPTER 5

DaaS Development

Abstract This chapter marks the first iteration of the applied ADR/eADR approach, focusing on problem-centric diagnosis to validate the research problem and lay the foundation for developing the envisaged *Bitcoin Audit Framework* (BTC_AF). Through collaborative engagement with the *1st Expert Team*, the chapter explores the integration of bitcoin into various sectors subject to statutory and regulatory audit requirements. The foundational artifact, the *Digital Asset Assertion Schedule* (DaaS), was developed using insights from practitioner workshops, which confirmed the complexities, risks, and knowledge gaps auditors face when auditing blockchain-based digital assets.

Key challenges identified include cryptographic verification, asset custody, and asset valuation across different business models. The DaaS confirms that current audit education and methodologies are insufficient and that a structured, adaptable framework is needed to support reliable audits of blockchain-based digital assets. As such, the DaaS serves as a critical problem validation artifact, highlighting the need for a systematic audit approach regarding management assertions about digital assets, thus shaping the design of the envisaged BTC_AF.

Keywords Audit • Asset custody • Asset valuation • Bitcoin • Blockchain • Cryptographic verification • Digital assets

JEL Classification M15 (IT Management): M42 (Auditing) • O31 (Innovation and Invention) • O33 (Technological Change)

W. Olivier, P. Buys, *Auditing Bitcoin*,
https://doi.org/10.1007/978-981-95-5775-2_5

5.1 Introduction

The previous chapter focused on auditing principles, contextualized in a blockchain environment. This chapter presents the first iteration of the *Bitcoin Audit Framework* (BTC_AF) development approach, focusing on validating the industry-experienced problem through engagement with the *1st Expert Team*. In doing so, it introduces the *Digital Asset Assertion Schedule* (DaaS) as the foundational artifact in the BTC_AF development.

5.2 Applied Design-Science Principles

As shown in Fig. 5.1, this iteration adopts an ADR-based diagnostic mindset, incorporating problem formulation, BIE activities, reflection, and formalization of learning stages as per Sein et al. (2011). This structured approach enables a thorough and rigorous examination of the research problem, forming a strong basis for later iterations.

The application of the above principles comes to fruition as follows: the literature review and insights gained during the *1st Expert Team* interactions serve to validate the relevance of the experienced problem, while the BIE stage, guided by reciprocal shaping and authentic assessment, involves collaborative development and iterative testing of proposed solutions, ensuring the DaaS evolves through real-world application. Next, the reflection incorporates feedback to refine the DaaS and support further development of BTC_AF. Finally, the formalized learning distills these insights into generalized outcomes that advance theory and practice in auditing both *Virtual Asset Service Providers* (VASPs) and non-VASPs that hold or transact with bitcoin.

5.3 Problem Formulation

The initial theoretical foundations provide the basis for addressing a practice-based problem and are grounded in contemporary technologies. In this book, problem formulation will be explored in collaboration with the *1st Expert Team* to validate industry observations on the integration of blockchain-based digital assets across various sectors.

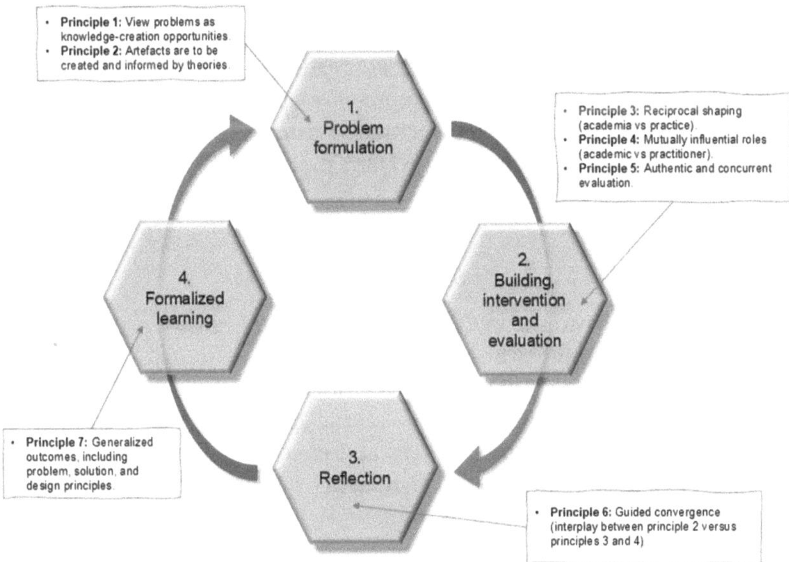

Fig. 5.1 Applied ADR principles. (Adapted from Sein et al. (2011))

5.3.1 Problem Revisited

The preceding chapters highlight the growing integration of blockchain-based digital assets into various sectors, including traditional finance. Organizations use these assets as a store of value and/or a medium of exchange, depending on their business models and industry dynamics (Puranam et al., 2019). The use of blockchain-based digital assets by VASPs and non-VASPs directly affects accounting records, and, in turn, the financial statements and audit opinions relied upon by relevant stakeholders.

In context, the complexity of blockchain-based assets demands auditors with expertise in blockchain technology, industry trends, and market behavior. Auditors must verify management's assertions regarding these assets, whether reflected as balances in the *Statement of Financial Position* (SoFP) or transactions in the *Statement of Profit and Loss* (SoPL), by obtaining sufficient and reliable evidence in line with *International Standards on Auditing* (ISA) requirements (Pelucio-Grecco et al., 2020).

Growing regulatory scrutiny further emphasizes the need for audits that adequately address associated risks.

Concerns persist regarding auditors' readiness to address these challenges, as knowledge gaps may compromise audit quality. The literature links ISA requirements to management's assertions regarding bitcoin-related balances and transactions, given its unique blockchain architecture and custody models.

5.3.2 Industry Corroboration

While literature provides context for the perceived industry problem, validating it through insights from industry experts is essential. This section outlines workshops held with the *1st Expert Team*, who were provided with background information, but specific literary details were downplayed to minimize confirmation bias and encourage objective feedback. The workshops explored six key themes to capture the complexities of auditing blockchain-based digital assets:

- Problem diagnosis: Integration of these assets into various *industrial* sectors and emerging business models.
- Financial reporting: Blockchain's role as a store of value, medium of exchange, and in custodial services.
- Regulatory landscape: Audit obligations for VASPs and non-VASPs engaging with blockchain-based digital assets.
- Technological perspective: Methods of custody and related audit difficulties.
- Audit perspective: Risks and challenges auditors face in this context.
- Solution perspective: Need for interdisciplinary expertise and structured audit programs.

These contextual themes validate the practical relevance of the envisaged BTC_AF and ensure it addresses real-world audit challenges. Although the BTC_AF will focus specifically on the Bitcoin blockchain, it also uses broader references to blockchain-based digital assets, reflecting their market dominance, as alluded to in Chap. 1.

The industry perspectives deepen the thematic classification and evaluation, as outlined in Table 5.1.

Table 5.1 Thematic analysis of industry perspectives

Theme	*Dimension*	*Summative Insight*
Problem Diagnosis	Sectoral Integration and Legacy System Constraints	Much integration is advancing in the financial sector utilizing blockchain-based digital assets for cross-border payments, trade finance, and crypto-linked investment products. Adoption in non-financial sectors is slower, notably in cross-border commerce and retail applications. A challenge is the difficulty organizations face when attempting to integrate blockchain-based assets within legacy systems, reflecting both technical and organizational barriers to broader adoption.
	Emergence of Blockchain-Native Business Models	VASPs have become central to the blockchain ecosystem, including crypto exchanges, custodians, and arbitrage traders. These entities provide core infrastructure: exchanges support trading, custodians ensure secure asset storage, and arbitrage traders improve liquidity. Bitcoin mining has also matured into a standalone industry, representing a new class of blockchain-native enterprises built entirely around the Bitcoin network.
Financial Reporting	Classification and Valuation Challenges	These assets have a significant impact on financial reporting, particularly when they are recorded on the balance sheet or used in transactions. Classification and valuation are complex due to volatility. Under IFRS and US GAAP, blockchain-based digital assets may be treated as intangible assets or inventory, but these frameworks may not fully reflect their dynamic nature.
	Suitability and Adaptation of IFRS	IFRS is applicable, but its application depends on the asset usage, i.e., for storage, transactions, speculation, or hedging. Adaptation is necessary to address the complexities of classification, valuation, and disclosure.

(*continued*)

Table 5.1 (continued)

Theme	*Dimension*	*Summative Insight*
Regulatory Landscape	Purpose and Scope of VASP Regulation	VASPs are increasingly regulated as authorities aim to integrate them into financial oversight frameworks. Regulators typically focus on solvency, financial stability, consumer protection, fraud prevention, AML compliance, and economic crime mitigation.
	Audit Requirements and Risk Considerations	Audit requirements generally stem from industry-specific regulations rather than exposure to the asset class alone. VASPs in the financial sector or listed companies may require audits. Still, due to the inherent risks associated with the asset class, stakeholders may request audits even if they are not legally required, emphasizing the importance of trust and transparency.
Technological Perspective	Custody Models and Risk Profiles	Assets are held via self-custody or third-party custody. Exchanges often use self-custody, employing multi-signature wallets. While self-custody offers control, it also carries risks, such as key mismanagement. Regulated third-party custodians provide enhanced security and are often preferred for institutional use. All assets ultimately remain on-chain, regardless of the method used.
	Auditor Competency Gaps	Auditors often lack the technical knowledge to audit blockchain-based assets effectively. Proficiency in blockchain mechanics, cryptographic verification, and on-chain analysis is usually missing from standard audit training, posing a significant capability gap.

(*continued*)

Table 5.1 (continued)

Theme	*Dimension*	*Summative Insight*
Audit Perspective	Inherent Risk and Complexity	Due to decentralization, volatility, and technical complexity, these assets pose high inherent risks. Auditors face challenges in verifying existence, ownership, and control—often without traditional documentation or intermediaries.
	Custody and Evidence Reliability	Custody models affect audit evidence requirements. Third-party custodians offer higher assurance through confirmations. Self-custody demands cryptographic verification, requiring greater expertise and skepticism.
	Specific Challenges	Verifying existence and ownership, especially under self-custody, and addressing valuation challenges due to volatility are primary concerns.
	Managing Risks	Effective mitigation requires specialized tools, revised procedures, and ongoing training. Leveraging regulated custodians and technical resources can improve audit reliability and confidence.
	Technological Barriers	Verifying cryptographic ownership, handling volatile prices, and the absence of intermediaries are key issues. Addressing these issues requires blockchain-specific tools and a deeper technical understanding.
	Audit Programs	Audit programs guide auditors in addressing key assertions and customizing procedures to risk areas. They support structured and consistent audit execution, enhancing the reliability of audit opinions.
Solution Perspective	Experience vs. Academic Learning	While academic learning provides a foundation, practical exposure is needed for cryptographic verification and blockchain-specific procedures, which are not typically covered in university programs.
	Preparedness of New Auditors	Traditional training often leaves gaps in key areas, such as ownership verification and blockchain tracing, rendering new auditors generally unprepared for blockchain-specific audit work.
	Interdisciplinary Collaboration	Auditing digital assets requires collaboration with IT and blockchain experts to bridge technical knowledge gaps and ensure the accuracy and completeness of audit evidence.
	Structured Audit Programs	A formal audit program can guide procedures for key assertions, standardize practices, and improve consistency and quality in digital asset assurance engagements.

5.4 Building, Intervention, and Evaluation

As indicated, the BIE stage involves the iterative development and refinement of the artifact through ongoing interaction with the problem domain. In the current iteration, the BIE focuses on developing the DaaS, drawing on insights from the *1st Expert Team*'s workshops and serving as a conceptual validation of the industry-experienced problem. The DaaS is derived from the integrative responses across the discussed themes, further distilled into the envisaged DaaS as presented in Table 5.2, providing the key concepts to consider.

The development of the DaaS reflected the principle of reciprocal shaping through an iterative, collaborative process with industry experts. It integrated feedback on the practical challenges of auditing blockchain-based digital assets across different business contexts. This ongoing interaction ensured the DaaS evolved with real-world insights, enhancing its relevance and grounding the envisaged BTC_AF in both theoretical and practical contexts.

The DaaS confirms the critical need for a relevant, structured framework and highlights the unique risks and complexities of auditing blockchain-based digital assets, now embedded across diverse business models. The DaaS marks a key milestone, guiding the next phase of BTC_AF development.

5.5 Reflection

The development of the DaaS marks a pivotal milestone in the BTC_AF development, reinforcing the central role of its design in addressing the audit challenges posed by blockchain-based digital assets. Rather than merely surfacing issues in abstract terms, the DaaS provides a structured mechanism through which related challenges are articulated, categorized, and evaluated in alignment with audit assertions. It bridges the gap between the conceptual understanding of blockchain-related audit complexities and the practical tools needed to address them in audit engagements.

Reflective engagement with industry practitioners revealed that auditors often lack the technical and procedural guidance necessary to verify assertions such as existence, rights, valuation, and completeness when auditing digital asset-related balances and transactions. The DaaS addressed this gap by integrating these assertions into the audit lifecycle for

Table 5.2 Digital asset audit schedule

Theme	*Key Elements*
Problem Diagnosis	• The use of blockchain-based digital assets is expanding across various industries. • Non-VASP business models and sectors are increasingly engaging with these assets. • Organizations dedicated to blockchain-based digital assets are becoming more sophisticated and widespread. • The rapid growth of VASPs highlights the emergence of a distinct sector built around this asset class and its technology.
Financial Reporting	• Blockchain-based digital asset transactions and balances affect financial reporting and accounting records when used as a medium of exchange or store of value by VASPs and non-VASPs. • IFRS is a globally recognized framework suitable for entities holding or transacting with these assets. • Digital assets may be classified as intangible assets at cost or as inventory at cost or fair value, depending on the business model.
Regulatory Landscape	• VASPs are subject to regulation, with oversight bodies often requiring independent audits to safeguard stakeholder interests. • Due to the complexity and risk, there is a growing demand for financial audits, even when not legally required, as stakeholders seek assurance over related financial reporting.
Technological Perspective	• Entities may use self-custody, third-party custodians, or a combination to hold blockchain-based digital assets. • Self-custody is common but carries higher risks, including key loss, mismanagement, or fraud. • Third-party custody simplifies audits, allowing auditors to rely on external confirmations, but introduces counterparty risk • Ultimately, all blockchain-based digital assets are held on-chain via self-custody mechanisms.

(*continued*)

Table 5.2 (continued)

Theme	*Key Elements*
Audit Perspective	• Auditing VASPs and non-VASPs that utilize blockchain-based assets involves a higher-than-normal risk. • Audit complexity differs between self-custody and third-party custody arrangements. • Third-party custody simplifies audits, allowing reliance on external confirmations. • Self-custody requires technical expertise in private key management, cryptographic verification of ownership, and balance verification. • A knowledge gap in the audit profession must be addressed to maintain audit quality and credibility. • Existing audit methodologies are inadequate for the unique challenges of blockchain-based assets. • There is a lack of structured tools and guidance tailored to auditing these assets. • Technical challenges exist, such as verifying ownership, navigating decentralized systems, and handling asset volatility and valuation. • The absence of intermediaries and traditional records complicates the collection of sufficient, reliable audit evidence. • Structured audit programs are essential to address management's assertions, regardless of asset type or category.
Solution Perspective	• Traditional audit education lacks coverage of the complexities of blockchain-based digital assets. • Even experienced auditors are often unprepared to navigate the intricacies of the asset class. • A structured audit program is needed to ensure sufficient and reliable evidence for blockchain-based digital assets.

organizations involved in blockchain-based digital assets, including both VASPs and non-VASPs. It enabled the structured identification of key risks, such as cryptographic verification, custody models, and valuation volatility. It translated them into a usable schedule that practitioners could relate to their professional environments.

Moreover, the DaaS serves as a boundary object, facilitating communication between auditors, blockchain experts, and researchers, and catalyzing co-reflection on both the limitations of existing audit methodologies and the characteristics required of an effective solution. The iterative co-construction of the DaaS exemplified reciprocal shaping, where practical insights informed theoretical refinement and vice versa.

While the eventual BTC_AF may take the form of a static framework, the DaaS demonstrated the need for dynamic interpretability, where artifacts must remain adaptable to evolving blockchain protocols, asset uses, and regulatory contexts. In this sense, the DaaS was not merely a precursor to the BTC_AF, but a foundational artifact that encapsulates the diagnostic learning phase and informs subsequent design iterations.

5.6 Formalized Learning

The formalization of learning in this iteration reflects the evolution of the DaaS from conceptual engagement to practical refinement. Through structured interactions with stakeholder groups and iterative feedback loops, insights were distilled into reusable knowledge assets. These include a decision-support framework that integrates key dimensions of Bitcoin's reality in an audit environment.

Key learning outcomes relate to the contextual sensitivity of DaaS implementations, specifically the need for organizations to align data utility with the expectations and governance structures of relevant actors. The iterative design process revealed that DaaS success is not solely driven by technological capability, but also by the social dynamics of trust, access control, and accountability within the data-sharing ecosystem.

The DaaS development further reinforced the role of guided emergence, where learning is shaped through real-world experimentation, and reciprocal shaping, where stakeholders actively influence artifact development. These principles contributed to an enriched understanding of how DaaS frameworks can be embedded within decision-making environments to improve responsiveness, transparency, and strategic alignment.

In formalizing these aspects, the artifact encapsulates not only a static model but also a transferable, adaptive tool that reflects the complex interplay of technical affordances and socio-organizational factors inherent in DaaS ecosystems.

5.7 Summary

This chapter focused on the problem-centric diagnosis phase of the ADR/eADR methodology, establishing the foundation for the BTC_AF. Through engagement with the *1st Expert Team* and analysis of industry insights, the research problem was systematically validated. The initial artifact, the DaaS, was developed iteratively to address key challenges in auditing blockchain-based digital assets. This includes aspects such as the audit profession's knowledge gap, the integration of assets into diverse business models, and the lack of structured guidance for reliable audit evidence.

The findings from this chapter further underscore the need for a practical and structured audit framework. The DaaS serves as a critical problem validation artifact, capturing practitioner perspectives and confirming the necessity of the BTC_AF. This collaborative, real-world approach ensured the DaaS's relevance and positioned it as a strong foundation for the BTC_AF's development.

These insights now lead into Chap. 6, where the initial, conceptual version of the BTC_AF will be developed.

References

Pelucio-Grecco, M. C., Santos Neto, J. P. D., & Constancio, D. (2020). Accounting for bitcoins in light of IFRS and tax aspects. *Revista Contabilidade & Finanças, 31*, 275–283.

Puranam, K. S. R., Gaddam, M. C. T., Panda, S. K., & Reddy, G. (2019, February). Anatomy and lifecycle of a bitcoin transaction. In *Proceedings of International Conference on Sustainable Computing in Science, Technology and Management (SUSCOM), Amity University Rajasthan, Jaipur-India*. https://ssrn.com/abstract=3355106

Sein, M. K., Henfridsson, O., Purao, S., Rossi, M., & Lindgren, R. (2011). Action design research. *MIS Quarterly, 35*(1), 37–56.

CHAPTER 6

BTC_AF$_{v1}$ Development

Abstract This chapter presents the development of BTC_AF$_{v1}$, the foundational iteration of the envisioned Bitcoin Audit Framework (BTC_AF), designed to guide auditors in addressing the complexities of auditing Bitcoin-related balances and transactions. Grounded in the object-centric design phase of the *elaborated Action Design Research* (eADR) methodology, the chapter responds to the book's objective through a structured framework aligned with *International Standards on Auditing* (ISA) assertions. Drawing on literature, practitioner insights, and the technical features of the Bitcoin blockchain protocol, the framework outlines detailed procedures that cover key areas, including wallet management, cryptographic ownership verification, and transactional completeness.

Each procedure is mapped to relevant assertions, ensuring audit rigor, clarity, and practical relevance. The result is a robust audit tool that integrates theoretical foundations with real-world application, offering clear guidance for auditors engaging with *Virtual Asset Service Providers* (VASPs) and non-VASPs exposed to the Bitcoin blockchain and its native currency. The BTC_AF$_{v1}$ thus establishes a foundation for industry validation, positioning itself as a valuable artifact in advancing audit quality and consistency within the evolving digital asset landscape.

Keywords Audit • Bitcoin • Blockchain protocol • Cryptographic verification • Digital assets • Elaborated action design research • International standards on auditing • Virtual asset service provider

W. Olivier, P. Buys, *Auditing Bitcoin*,
https://doi.org/10.1007/978-981-95-5775-2_6

JEL Classification M15 (IT Management): M42 (Auditing) • O31 (Innovation and Invention) • O33 (Technological Change)

6.1 Introduction

Through the development of the *Digital Asset Audit Schedule* (DaaS), the previous chapter validated the targeted problem as a real, industry-experienced issue. This chapter responds by developing a baseline *Bitcoin Audit Framework* (BTC_AF) as part of the eADR object-centric design iteration. This framework serves as a structured audit program with detailed explanations, guiding auditors in obtaining sufficient and appropriate audit evidence for contextual management assertions related to balances and transactions.

6.2 Applied Design-Science Principles

The object-centric design iteration focuses on developing the BTC_AF_{v1} artifact, which is formulated by combining theoretical insights with practical needs identified during the development of the DaaS. In line with the defined design methodology, this iteration also follows the four ADR stages, as per Sein et al. (2011):

- Problem formulation: Refines the envisaged BTC_AF_{v1}'s scope and objectives based on earlier findings, clearly outlining the audit challenges it must address to close the knowledge gap.
- Building, intervention, and evaluation: The artifact is iteratively developed and enhanced using practitioner feedback.
- Reflection: Assesses the artifact's real-world relevance and effectiveness, identifying areas for improvement and clarifying the principles behind its impact.
- Formalized learning: Consolidates the knowledge gained, ensuring the BTC_AF_{v1} is both practical and theoretically sound.

This structured, iterative approach should ensure the envisaged BTC_AF is robust, relevant, and capable of guiding auditors in engagements involving the Bitcoin blockchain and its native currency.

6.3 Problem Revisited

As outlined in earlier chapters, the integration of blockchain-based digital assets into the global economy has introduced significant challenges for auditors. Used as a store of value and/or medium of exchange, these assets impact financial records and therefore require auditors to critically assess management's assertions and gather sufficient, reliable evidence in line with *International Standards on Auditing* (ISA). However, the technical complexity of the Bitcoin blockchain, including its cryptographic controls, decentralized systems, and market volatility, makes this task challenging. As regulatory expectations rise and digital assets become more integrated into various business models, auditors must adopt a structured approach that aligns with the ISA while addressing the unique attributes of the Bitcoin blockchain and its native currency.

The DaaS is a foundational artifact designed to validate the actuality of the problem and inform the development of the BTC_AF$_{v1}$. Developed through thematic analysis and collaboration with the *1st Expert Team*, this approach addresses key challenges in auditing bitcoin. These include integrating such assets into business models, applying *International Financial Reporting Standards* (IFRS), navigating regulatory maturity for both *Virtual Asset Service Providers* (VASPs) and non-VASPs, managing custody complexities, and understanding the intricacies of technology. The theme integration highlights the widespread adoption of blockchain-based digital assets across sectors, adding complexity to audit procedures. In this context, the *financial reporting* theme examines the challenges of applying IFRS, particularly in valuing, classifying, and disclosing these assets. The *regulatory* theme highlights gaps in oversight and audit expectations, thereby complicating auditors' responsibilities. The *technological* theme addresses the challenges of verifying existence, ownership, and custody. In contrast, the *audit perspective* theme stresses the need for clear guidance to address emerging risks and evidence requirements that will support the audit opinion.

Ultimately, the DaaS highlights a knowledge gap in the audit profession and underscores the need for a structured framework to enhance audit quality, reliability, and consistency in this evolving area.

6.4 Building, Intervention, and Evaluation

Guided by reciprocal shaping, the BTC_AF$_{v1}$ evolves in response to audit challenges associated with the Bitcoin blockchain and its native currency. The principle of mutually influential roles emphasizes the collaborative engagement between researcher and practitioner teams in shaping the artifacts. The BTC_AF$_{v1}$ framework builds on established audit assertions, contextualized by the DaaS. As such, the audit procedures are structured into three categories: General information, which provides foundational contexts; the *Statement of Financial Position* (SoFP); and the *Statement of Profit and Loss* (SoPL), which targets specific assertions to secure sufficient and reliable audit evidence for balances and transactions. This structure enables a comprehensive response to the complexities of auditing bitcoin as a blockchain-based digital asset.

6.4.1 General Information

In terms of the general information requirements, the following procedures are suggested:

- **Procedure 1:** Inquire whether management holds bitcoin through self-custody (on-chain), a third-party custodian, or a combination of both. This information guides the extent of audit procedures required. When a third-party custodian is used, management should be able to provide an independent statement confirming the entity's bitcoin holdings at year-end, which includes the entity's name, financial year-end, and nominal balance(s). This generally covers most audit assertions, except for valuation and presentation/disclosure, which can be tested similarly to self-custodied holdings. If self-custody is used, additional audit procedures are necessary, as detailed in the subsequent procedures.
- **Procedure 2:** Inquire whether management uses a *hierarchical deterministic* (HD) wallet structure to manage their Bitcoin addresses. If so, obtain the wallet's xpub, associated addresses, and their derivation paths. This enables the auditor to utilize BIP 32 keys and derivation paths to identify all related child public keys, addresses, and transactions, thereby enhancing assurance over the completeness of management's reported Bitcoin addresses, in conjunction with *Information Produced by the Entity* (IPE) procedures.

- **Procedure 3:** Inquire with management about the blockchain cut-off date and time or block height used in their accounting policy for financial reporting (e.g., 31 December 2023, 23:59:59 UTC or block 823,785). Where the accounting policy refers to a specific block height (e.g., 823,785) as the reporting cut-off, the auditor must assess whether this block height aligns with the financial reporting period and the financial statements as a whole. As each blockchain block within the blockchain includes a timestamp and block height, and because the Bitcoin network operates continuously, this ensures that all relevant transactions are captured in line with the entity's reporting time and date. In group structures, the auditor must also verify consistent application of the cut-off time and date to prevent double-counting across related entities.

6.4.2 SoFP Procedures

Based on the SoFP requirements, the following procedures are proposed:

- **Procedure 4:** Obtain management's schedule detailing nominal bitcoin balances per address and their functional currency values. Verify that the total functional currency balance aligns with the general ledger, trial balance, and financial statements. This confirms consistency between the schedule and reported figures and provides a list of addresses for retrieving transactional data from a full node to build year-end balances. Note that assessing the completeness of this schedule falls under IPE procedures and is outside the BTC_AF's scope.
- **Procedure 5:** For each address in management's schedule, use a transactional harvesting and aggregation tool to query a full Bitcoin node and confirm the nominal balance as of the financial reporting date and time. This verifies that the claimed *Unspent Transaction Output* (UTXO) balances exist within the listed addresses. The tool, which accesses the complete transaction history of the address via the full node, returns balances aligned with the entity's reporting period. These are compared against management's schedule to validate accuracy and identify discrepancies. While the BTC_AF does not cover evaluating the tool itself, auditors must consider its independence and reliability, as outdated or biased sources can produce inaccurate results. Any differences should be discussed with management

and addressed appropriately based on materiality and audit risk assessments.

- **Procedure 6:** If management uses an HD wallet structure, use the provided xpub and a BIP 32 deterministic key generator tool to derive child keys along the relevant derivation paths. Convert these keys into Bitcoin addresses using a pubkey-to-address conversion tool, then apply the transactional harvesting and aggregation tool to determine their nominal balances, as outlined in Procedure 5. Compare the resulting addresses with management's schedule to assess completeness. The BIP 32 tool, utilizing the xpub and variable derivation paths, enables the auditor to confirm or re-perform management's process, generating an extended list of addresses to ensure that all UTXO-holding addresses linked to the xpub are captured. This approach supports validation of address completeness and associated balances.
- **Procedure 7:** If management uses a hybrid custodian, such as a cryptocurrency exchange, to convert bitcoin to fiat, other digital assets, or *vice versa*, obtain the entity's transaction history from the hybrid custodian for the relevant financial period. Identify all send/receive transactions involving the hybrid custodian and other Bitcoin addresses and inquire about any unidentified addresses to detect potential omissions from management's provided list of Bitcoin addresses and balances. This helps the auditor confirm the completeness of management's address schedule by comparing transaction counterparties with the reported addresses. Any unmatched addresses should be supported by documentation and/or explanation. Note that validating the accuracy and completeness of data from the hybrid custodian is part of IPE procedures and lies outside the BTC_AF's scope.
- **Procedure 8:** Using management's schedule of Bitcoin addresses and balances, reconciled with the trial balance and financial statements, recalculating the functional currency values based on the spot price of bitcoin and the applicable accounting policy at period-end. This determines the accuracy of fair value reporting on the SoFP or potential impairment indicators. The auditor must assess whether a fair value or cost basis was applied and ensure the spot rate aligns with the policy's cut-off date/time and is drawn from a reliable, independent source. The auditor should also consider bitcoin's market liquidity and any jurisdictional factors that may cause price devia-

tions. While evaluation of spot rate sources and IPE-related checks fall outside the BTC_AF's scope, any discrepancies should be discussed with management and addressed according to materiality, audit methodology, and the relevant accounting framework.

- **Procedure 9:** Inquire whether management's Bitcoin addresses are single-signature or multi-signature. This distinction is essential for determining the appropriate audit approach to verify control and ownership. Single-signature addresses require a single private key for access, whereas multi-signature addresses involve multiple keys and shared control. For multi-signature addresses, the auditor must confirm that the necessary m-of-n signing threshold is valid. This understanding ensures the auditor applies the correct testing procedures, improving the accuracy and reliability of audit results.
- **Procedure 10:** Inquire whether management can perform cryptographic message signing on their single- and/or multi-signature addresses. This helps the auditor assess management's ability to demonstrate knowledge of the private key(s) associated with each public key(s) and the corresponding address listed in their schedule. If message signing isn't possible, an alternative procedure, such as a "send to self" transaction, as outlined in Procedure 13, should be followed.
- **Procedure 11:** Generate a unique, random phrase that includes numbers, letters, and special characters, and provide it to management. Request that they cryptographically sign it using the private key associated with the address under audit. Management then submits the signature to the audit team for verification, as outlined in Procedure 12. This demonstrates management's knowledge of the private key associated with the address listed in their schedule, confirming control. The exact phrase may be reused for multiple addresses, at the auditor's discretion.
- **Procedure 12:** Use a cryptographic message verification tool to validate the signature provided by management. Input the address being tested, the unique message, and the cryptographic signature, obtained in procedure 11, into the tool. The Bitcoin protocol's deterministic algorithms verify whether the signature was generated by the private key associated with the address, without revealing the key itself. This process verifies that management controls the private key, providing assurance of ownership over the address and its associated funds.

- **Procedure 13:** If management cannot perform cryptographic message signing, request them to sweep the entire balance from the address in question to another address they control and provide the transaction hash. This on-chain transaction demonstrates control by requiring the private key linked to the original address. To prevent manipulation, the auditor should avoid partial transfers (e.g., Satoshi tests) and may introduce randomness, such as short notice or in-person observation, to confirm the transaction's authenticity. The transaction hash and its details can then be verified using a blockchain explorer connected to a full node.
- **Procedure 14:** If management's list includes multi-signature addresses, obtain the m-of-n configuration for each multi-signature address as well as the corresponding "m" public keys required to authorize transactions for each of these addresses. This helps the auditor understand the threshold of necessary signatories and the public keys involved. With this information, the auditor can design appropriate procedures to verify that each required signatory controls their respective private key, ensuring proper control and security over the multi-sig addresses.
- **Procedure 15:** For each multi-signature address in management's list, use a blockchain explorer linked to a full node to locate an output transaction that reveals the m-of-n signature setup. Retrieve the P2SH Redeem Script from the transaction and compare it with the configuration provided by management. Convert each of the "m" public keys into Bitcoin addresses using a pubkey-to-address tool and perform ownership testing as outlined in Procedures 11 and/or 13. This process verifies that the disclosed m-of-n setup is accurate and confirms each signatory's control, ensuring the integrity and security of the multi-signature configuration. For multi-signature addresses, it is only necessary to perform ownership testing on the minimum number of public keys required to meet the signature threshold (e.g., any two of three in a 2-of-3 configuration).
- **Procedure 16:** If the entity uses an HD wallet structure with multiple addresses derived from a single xpub, the auditor can test ownership of one associated address, i.e., the target address, to verify control over the entire structure. Using the xpub, the target address, and its derivation path, apply a BIP 32 deterministic key generator and pubkey-to-address tool to reproduce the target address, confirming its link to the xpub. This demonstrates that the address is

part of the HD wallet, and successful ownership testing (as per Procedures 11 and/or 13) assures all addresses derived from the xpub.

- **Procedure 17:** The auditor must ensure that the entity's bitcoin holdings are appropriately accounted for and disclosed according to its accounting policy and the applicable financial reporting framework. While this procedure lies outside the BTC_AF's scope, due to its reliance on the specific framework, policy, and entity type, it supports the auditor in addressing the classification, presentation, and disclosure assertion.

6.4.3 SoPL Procedures

To meet the requirements of the SoPL, the following procedures should be undertaken:

- **Procedure 18:** Inquire whether management's schedule includes controlled addresses with no UTXOs (spent or empty addresses), as some may have been thoroughly used during the financial period. If not included, request an updated schedule and/or use the xpub to identify all linked addresses if the client plans to use HD wallets. Subject any additional spent addresses to ownership testing as outlined in Procedures 11, 13, and/or 17. Together with Procedure 7, this helps confirm the completeness of management's address list and verifies the entity's control over all addresses used for transactions throughout the financial period under review.
- **Procedure 19:** Use the transaction harvesting and aggregation tool to retrieve all transactions linked to the addresses in management's updated schedule and/or the xpub for the financial period. This provides the auditor with a complete, immutable record of transactions executed and received by addresses under the entity's control. Transactions involving hybrid or dedicated custodians are outside the scope of the BTC_AF.
- **Procedure 20:** Inquire with management about which general ledger or trial balance accounts were used for recording the sending or receiving of bitcoin-related payments. This helps the auditor understand how bitcoin transactions are reflected in the financial records and identify accounts that record interaction with the Bitcoin blockchain.

- **Procedure 21:** For each bitcoin-associated account identified in Procedure 20, reconcile the complete transaction listing (or sample) with transactions from the addresses in management's schedule used for sending or receiving bitcoin. This confirms that all blockchain transactions are accurately recorded in the financial accounts (completeness) and that the recorded transactions occurred (occurrence) on the blockchain. The procedure also addresses cut-off by comparing blockchain timestamps with the reporting period. Any mismatches may indicate missing, misclassified, or misdated transactions.
- **Procedure 22:** Use the transaction harvesting and aggregation tool to obtain all bitcoin transactions linked to the addresses in management's schedule for the financial period. Reconcile these, either entirely or on a sample basis, by converting the nominal bitcoin amounts to the functional currency using the applicable spot rate. Compare the converted values to related income and expense entries in the general ledger to ensure accurate SoPL reporting following the entity's accounting policy and framework. This procedure confirms the completeness and accuracy of bitcoin-related income and expenses, with any variances assessed against materiality, audit methodology, and relevant standards. Refer to Procedure 8 for related considerations.

6.5 Reflection

The BTC_AF$_{v1}$ is the initial iteration of the envisaged audit framework developed in this research, designed in line with the design science criteria of Hevner et al. (2004) to ensure preliminary validity. Although it has not yet undergone the verification and validation processes scheduled in subsequent iterations, it forms a solid foundation for future refinement. BTC_AF$_{v1}$ will be reassessed against verification and validation design statements to ensure it effectively addresses the complexities of auditing VASPs and non-VASPs exposed to bitcoin.

As a structured audit approach, the BTC_AF$_{v1}$ will endeavor to operate independently of personnel or organizations, providing auditors with a systematic framework for obtaining reliable evidence in blockchain-related engagements. It addresses a critical gap in audit practice by aligning audit standards with the unique attributes of the Bitcoin blockchain. Its value lies in its clear, theory-based structure, ensuring understandability for auditors with limited blockchain expertise.

The framework, therefore, contributes to audit practice by bridging theory and real-world applications, offering a model for auditing emerging technologies. Its development is based on rigorous data collection, including literature reviews, practitioner workshops, and empirical insights. The BTC_AF$_{v1}$ also reflects a design-as-exploration process, shaped through iterative feedback and aligned with verification criteria. Structured for clear communication, it supports adoption by auditors and other legitimate stakeholders.

Together, these elements affirm the BTC_AF$_{v1}$'s status as a valid design science artefact and a significant contribution to advancing audit practices in the context of bitcoin-related transactions and balances.

6.6 Formalized Learning

The formalization of learning consolidates the BTC_AF$_{v1}$ into a structured framework tailored to audit bitcoin-related balances and transactions, ensuring each procedure aligns with key audit assertions (see Table 6.1).

By mapping procedures to the assertions of the SoFP and SoPL, the formalization validates the framework's design and functionality, demonstrating both its practical utility and theoretical soundness. Hence, the BTC_AF$_{v1}$ conceptual framework, shown in Fig. 6.1, presents a holistic

Table 6.1 Audit assertion map

	Statement of Financial Position					Statement of Profit and Loss			
	Procedure	Existence	Rights and Ownership	Completeness	Valuation	Accuracy	Cut-off	Occurrence	Completeness
General	1	N/A	N/A	N/A	N/A	N/A	N/A	N/A	N/A
	2	N/A	N/A	N/A	N/A	N/A	N/A	N/A	N/A
	3	N/A	N/A	N/A	N/A	N/A	N/A	N/A	N/A
Statement of Financial Position	4	-	-	X	X	N/A	N/A	N/A	N/A
	5	X	-	X	X	N/A	N/A	N/A	N/A
	6	X	-	X	X	N/A	N/A	N/A	N/A
	7	-	-	X	-	N/A	N/A	N/A	N/A
	8	-	-	-	X	N/A	N/A	N/A	N/A
	9	N/A	N/A	N/A	N/A	N/A	N/A	N/A	N/A
	10	N/A	N/A	N/A	N/A	N/A	N/A	N/A	N/A
	11	-	X	-	-	N/A	N/A	N/A	N/A
	12	-	X	-	-	N/A	N/A	N/A	N/A
	13	-	X	-	-	N/A	N/A	N/A	N/A
	14	-	X	-	-	N/A	N/A	N/A	N/A
	15	-	X	-	-	N/A	N/A	N/A	N/A
	16	-	X	-	-	N/A	N/A	N/A	N/A
	17	N/A	N/A	N/A	N/A	N/A	N/A	N/A	N/A
Statement of Profit and Loss	18	N/A	N/A	N/A	N/A	-	-	-	X
	19	N/A	N/A	N/A	N/A	-	-	-	X
	20	N/A	N/A	N/A	N/A	N/A	N/A	N/A	N/A
	21	N/A	N/A	N/A	N/A	-	X	X	X
	22	N/A	N/A	N/A	N/A	X	-	-	-

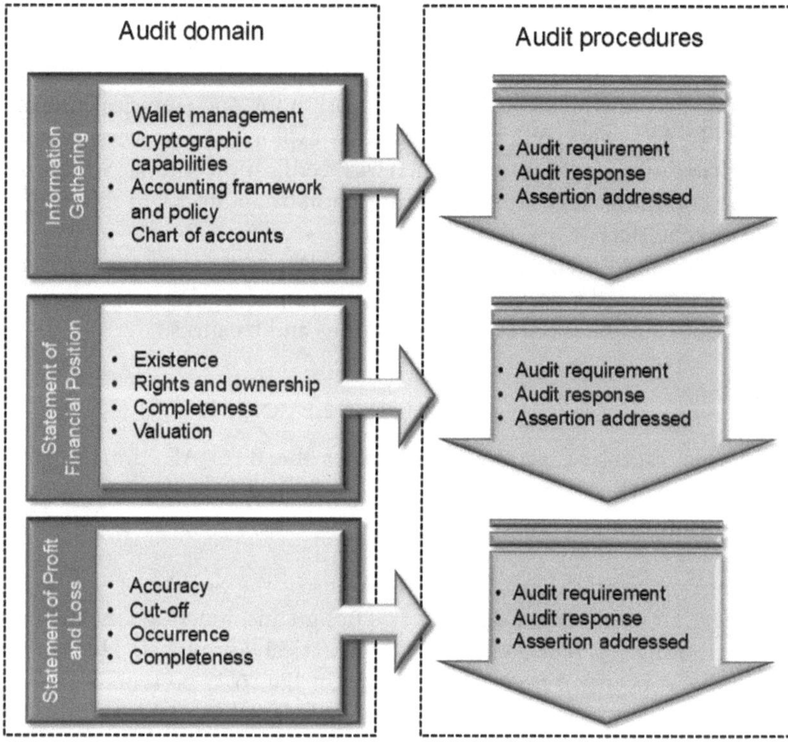

Fig. 6.1 BTC_AF$_{v1}$ conceptual framework

view of its design, shaped by reflection and learning from the BIE stage of the ADR process. This ensures the framework meets the audit profession's specific needs while establishing a strong basis for its validation and future refinement.

The BTC_AF$_{v1}$ framework begins with an *information-gathering* phase that forms the foundation for all subsequent SoFP and SoPL audit procedures. In this phase, the auditor collects key details on wallet management, cryptographic capabilities, accounting policies, and financial record structures. These insights are crucial for tailoring the audit approach to the specific risks associated with the Bitcoin blockchain and its native currency, reflecting the iterative learning from the BIE stage. The framework then addresses the key assertions for the *SoFP*, i.e., existence, rights and obligations, completeness, and valuation, and for the *SoPL*, accuracy, cut-off, occurrence, and completeness. These assertions, rooted in the initial phase, guide the design of procedures that align with ISA standards and the technical demands of auditing bitcoin.

Each procedure in the BTC_AF$_{v1}$ is mapped to its relevant assertion, detailing the audit requirement, response, and intended outcome. This structured, assertion-driven approach ensures consistency, clarity, and audit reliability, reinforcing the framework's adaptability and effectiveness in supporting audit opinions.

6.7 Summary

This chapter marks a critical step in addressing the complexities of auditing bitcoin-related balances and transactions through the development of BTC_AF$_{v1}$. Grounded in the object-centric design iteration of the ADR/eADR approach, the framework's construction links each procedure to the relevant SoFP and SoPL assertions. By aligning audit requirements, responses, and assertions, the BTC_AF will aim to offer a robust and adaptable structure tailored to the unique challenges of auditing bitcoin-associated balances and transactions. This chapter demonstrated the integration of theoretical rigor with practical insights, equipping auditors with a reliable tool. The next chapter will advance to the BTC_AF's validation-centric iteration as per the ADR/eADR framework.

References

Hevner, A. R., March, S. T., & Park, J. (2004). Design science in information systems research. *MIS Quarterly, 28*(1), 75–105.

Sein, M. K., Henfridsson, O., Purao, S., Rossi, M., & Lindgren, R. (2011). Action design research. *MIS Quarterly, 35*(1), 37–56.

CHAPTER 7

BTC_AF$_{v2}$ Validation

Abstract This chapter builds on the foundations established in earlier chapters, integrating feedback from the *2nd Expert Team* to validate and enhance the framework's practical applicability and theoretical rigor. Through structured workshops and in-depth analysis, the team evaluated the first version of the *Bitcoin Audit Framework* (BTC_AF) against key verification and validation statements, assessing its alignment with *International Standards on Auditing* (ISA) and its ability to address the unique complexities of auditing bitcoin-related digital asset balances and transactions.

Although key refinements were introduced to improve the framework's functionality, insights from practitioners that did not require structural changes were recorded for discussion in later chapters. The iterative nature of this stage reinforces the importance of learning and adaptation in artifact development. The BTC_AF$_{v1}$ was further assessed against key design science criteria, confirming its value as a theoretically grounded, practically applicable audit tool. The chapter concludes by positioning BTC_AF$_{v2}$ as a validated artifact capable of supporting auditors in navigating the audit challenges posed by blockchain technologies, with its real-world implementation to follow in the next phase.

Keywords Audit challenges • Bitcoin • Blockchain technology • Design science • Digital assets • International standards on auditing

JEL Classification M15 (IT Management): M42 (Auditing) • O31 (Innovation and Invention) • O33 (Technological Change)

W. Olivier, P. Buys, *Auditing Bitcoin*,
https://doi.org/10.1007/978-981-95-5775-2_7

7.1 Introduction

This chapter marks a pivotal phase in the development of the envisaged *Bitcoin Audit Framework* (BTC_AF), as it transitions from its initial development to its validation. Building on the previous chapter's BTC_AF_{v1}, the *2nd Expert Team* is introduced to verify and validate the framework against the earlier defined design statements. Through structured discussions and in-depth analysis, this team will assess the framework's alignment with key audit assertions and the *International Standards on Auditing* (ISA). They will offer insights into its practical relevance, strengths, and areas for improvement, culminating in a validated BTC_AF.

7.2 Applied Design-Science Principles

In line with the design methodology, the current iteration also applies the four ADR stages as per Sein et al. (2011). In context, the problem formulation stage sharpens the BTC_AF_{v1}'s scope by refining audit challenges. In contrast, the building, intervention, and evaluation stages focus on iterative development guided by practitioner feedback and theoretical insights. The reflection stage assesses real-world relevance, clarifies underlying principles, and identifies improvements. Finally, the formalized learning stage consolidates knowledge to ensure BTC_AF is both practical and theoretically robust.

Ultimately, the feedback from industry practitioners will guide the refinement of the framework into a validated, practitioner-informed BTC_AFv2, laying the foundation for its implementation in real-world contexts.

7.3 Problem Revisited

As a blockchain-based digital asset, bitcoin is increasingly being integrated across various sectors, posing unique challenges for auditors in substantiating management's assertions (Bo & Wu, 2011; Tian and Xin, 2017). When presented as balances or transactions in the *Statement of Financial Position* (SoFP) and the *Statement of Profit and Loss* (SoPL), auditors must obtain sufficient and reliable evidence per ISA requirements (Meleschenko et al., 2020). This involves addressing key assertions while navigating the Bitcoin blockchain and its native currency's complex architecture, cryptographic design, and market dynamics. Bitcoin's decentralized and pseudonymous nature, along with its technical complexity, requires specialized expertise and tailored audit approaches. A volatile market and evolving regulations (Baur and Dimpfl, 2021) further compound these challenges, reinforcing the need for robust audit practices to ensure reliable financial reporting for entities engaging with bitcoin.

7.4 Build, Intervention, and Evaluation

The BIE stage in the applied ADR/eADR process remains central. Through iterative reflection and learning, this stage enhances the framework's ability to address the complexities of gaining audit evidence related to bitcoin balances and transactions. The *2nd Expert Team* will review the DaaS to confirm its relevance to both theoretical and practical audit needs. They will evaluate BTC_AFv1 against the verification and validation statements to assess its alignment with audit assertions and practical use, as shown in Fig. 7.1.

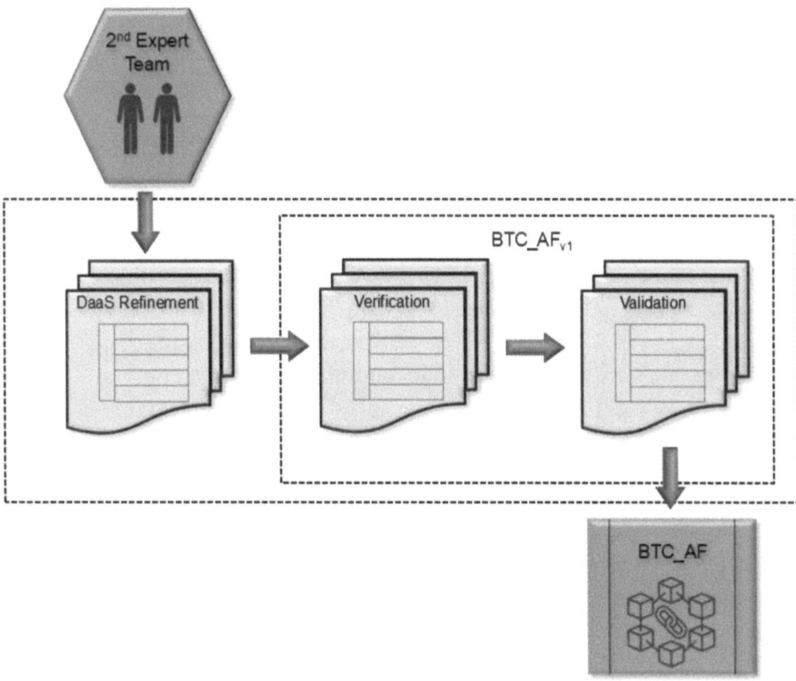

Fig. 7.1 Refinement, verification, and validation process

As indicated, there may be room for potential improvement and refinement opportunities to the DaaS and the envisaged BTC_AF. The illustrated actions are elaborated in the sections below.

7.4.1 DaaS Refinement

The DaaS, shared with the *2nd Expert Team*, provides a diagnostic foundation by outlining key challenges and knowledge gaps in auditing blockchain-based digital assets. Developed from prior workshops and literature, this framework offers a conceptual basis and invites further input from the team.

The *2nd Expert Team* confirmed that the DaaS effectively captures the integration of bitcoin as a digital asset into various business models and the key challenges faced by the audit profession. They validated its relevance and affirmed the need for a structured audit framework.

7.4.2 BTC_AF Verification

This section assesses the applicability of the BTC_AF_{v1} design against key verification (design) statements, focusing on key audit assertions, i.e., has the framework been designed in a manner cognizant of the foundational audit assertions of existence, rights and obligations, completeness, accuracy, valuation, cut-off, and occurrence. The summative results are presented in Table 7.1.

Feedback from the *2nd Expert Team* was crucial for refining the framework and ensuring its alignment with ISA, particularly regarding the technological aspects of the Bitcoin blockchain. This iterative process informed the verification of the BTC_AF design by identifying strengths, areas for improvement, and additional enhancements to increase the framework's robustness.

7.4.3 BTC_AF Validation

The validation process aims to determine whether BTC_AF_{v1} effectively addresses the practical challenges of auditing bitcoin-related balances and transactions. Using key validation (design) statements, the *2nd Expert Team* will evaluate the framework's ability to guide auditors in obtaining sufficient and reliable audit evidence. The summative results are presented in Table 7.2.

Table 7.1 BTC_AF verification

	Requirement	*Verification response*
Existence	Obtain sufficient and reliable evidence to verify the existence of bitcoin balances.	It is confirmed that it effectively supports the existence assertion by providing a structured method to verify the existence of bitcoin balances, whether custodian-held or within a self-custody solution. While concerns remain about reliance on 3rd party custodians given the lack of regulatory oversight, the framework offers a strong foundation for auditing the existence of regulations as they continue to evolve.
Rights and obligations	Obtain reliable evidence that management has enforceable rights to the custodied bitcoin, or control over private key(s) for the relevant wallet or address in the case of self-custody.	Although it was confirmed that it effectively addresses the rights and obligations assertion and provides reliable guidance for verifying control and ownership, it was suggested to add ownership references, date, purpose, and a recent block hash to the message subjected to cryptographic message signing. In multi-signature cases, challenges may arise when clients provide only a derived address without public keys, and when the redeem script is unavailable, complicating verification of thresholds and associated keys.
Completeness	Obtain evidence to confirm that management's reported Bitcoin addresses appear in the SoFP and that all related transactions are recorded in the SoPL.	It is confirmed that it effectively addresses the completeness assertion, offering a structured approach to ensure reported addresses and transactions are thoroughly and accurately recorded in the SoFP and SoPL. The procedures provide sufficient guidance for obtaining supporting evidence, with no further enhancements needed.

(continued)

Table 7.1 (continued)

	Requirement	*Verification response*
Accuracy and valuation	Obtain reliable evidence that bitcoin balances in the SoFP and transactions in the SoPL are accurately measured in the functional currency and accounted for in terms of the relevant accounting framework.	It is confirmed that it adequately addresses the accuracy and valuation assertion, guiding auditors in measuring bitcoin balances and transactions with spot prices. One member recommended using a regulated price index to strengthen credibility.
Cut-off	Obtain sufficient evidence to confirm that all bitcoin-related transactions in the SoPL are recorded in the correct period.	It is confirmed that it effectively addresses the cut-off assertion, offering clear guidance to ensure bitcoin transactions are recorded in the correct period. While all agreed the procedures are sufficient, one suggested using block height for greater precision than timestamps, given their variability; however, this was refuted based on the premise that blockchain data must conform with conventional reporting timelines, which the utilization of the relevant harvesting and aggregation tools should facilitate.
Occurrence	Obtain sufficient evidence to confirm that bitcoin-related payments or receipts impacting the SoPL have occurred.	It is confirmed that it fully addresses the occurrence assertion, providing clear procedures for auditors to verify transactions through their recording on the Bitcoin blockchain, with no further suggestions.

As the ultimate phase in the iterative BTC_AF development, the industry validation helped fine-tune the framework's practical applicability and support in the context of bitcoin auditing.

7.4.4 *Summary of Refinements*

The response from the *2nd Expert Team* was evaluated to determine whether no action was needed, if best practice enhancements could be made without altering the core framework, or if refinements were

Table 7.2 BTC_AF validation

Requirement	*Validation response*
Use the BTC_AF to align procedures with the Bitcoin blockchain's technical and market complexities while ensuring sufficient and reliable audit evidence.	Confirmed that it enables auditors to address Bitcoin's technical complexities and design effective procedures to obtain reliable evidence.
Use BTC_AF to validate management's assertions regarding bitcoin balances and transactions, assuring the audit opinion.	Confirmed that it supports practical audit procedures to substantiate management's assertions with sufficient and reliable evidence.
Apply BTC_AF as an effective program to assure bitcoin balances in the SoFP and transactions in the SoPL.	The framework is validated as a systematic audit program that assures relevant assertions, aligns with standards, and ensures comprehensive coverage.

Table 7.3 Impact summary

	No action required	*Best practice*	*Refinement of the BTC_AF$_{v2}$*
DaaS	X		
Verification Statements			
• Existence	X		
• Rights and obligations		X	X
• Completeness	X		
• Accuracy and valuation	X		
• Cut-off	X		
• Occurrence	X		
Verification statements	N/A	N/A	N/A

necessary to evolve into BTC_AF. Table 7.3 summarizes such feedback and indicates its impact on key aspects of the framework.

As indicated, the refinement targeted actionable improvements that enhance the framework's functionality, such as updating Procedure 15 (as part of the Rights and Obligations assertion) to address multi-signature (multi-sig) setups, ensuring the BTC_AF can manage complex audit scenarios.

7.5 Reflection

This stage marks a crucial phase in the artifact's iterative development, driven by feedback and validation insights focused on real-world applicability and addressing identified gaps. This was achieved through structured engagement with the *2nd Expert Team*, whose input directly informed the BTC_AF_{v2} refinement.

Practitioner engagement through targeted discussions and workshops highlighted practical challenges, particularly in accessing inputs for certain validation procedures. These insights guided specific refinements to improve the framework's usability and applicability, reinforcing the value of continuous feedback in aligning the framework with both theoretical standards and audit practice. The refinement process reflected an iterative cycle of reflection and learning, systematically integrating practitioner input to strengthen the framework. This effectively demonstrated Principle 6 of the ADR framework, i.e., the importance of iterative feedback in artifact development (Mullarkey & Hevner, 2018; Sein et al., 2011). These refinements and best practice applications are included and illustrated in Chap. 8.

7.6 Formalized Learning

Consolidating insights and feedback into a refined, validated artifact ensures the culmination of iterative learning aligned with the principles of the ADR/eADR framework. Hevner et al. (2004) established criteria for evaluating artifacts in design science research, ensuring theoretical rigor, practical relevance, and field contribution. The BTC_AF_{v2} is assessed against these criteria through the verification and validation statements, demonstrating its ability to address the complexities of auditing bitcoin-related balances and transactions. This alignment affirms the artifact's robustness, adaptability, and readiness for real-world use. The evaluation below outlines how each of Hevner's criteria is met:

- Construct, Model, Method, or Instantiation: The BTC_AF_{v2} is a structured audit framework that integrates theory with practical audit application, confirmed by practitioner validation.
- Business Problem Addressed: It addresses audit challenges related to bitcoin-associated transactions and balances, equipping auditors to operate within ISA standards.

- Functionality, Performance, Reliability, Usability: Designed for usability and audit effectiveness, the BTC_AF$_{v2}$ has been validated for real-world readiness and adaptability.
- Research Contribution: The BTC_AF$_{v2}$ represents a novel contribution to auditing bitcoin-related balances and transactions, bridging academic theory with practice.
- Rigor in Development: The framework was built using rigorous methods, including literature review, thematic analysis, and structured practitioner feedback.
- Stakeholder Communication: It was communicated and well-received by practitioners through structured workshops, confirming its accessibility and practical relevance.

Through this evaluation, the BTC_AF$_{v2}$ is positioned as a validated artifact suitable for real-world audit environments. The formalization process illustrates how iterative refinement shaped the anticipated BTC_AF into a practitioner-informed, theoretically grounded framework.

7.7 Summary

This chapter detailed the iterative verification and validation of the BTC_AF$_{v2}$, evolving it from BTC_AF$_{v1}$ into the practitioner-informed BTC_AF$_{v2}$. Through structured engagement with the *2nd Expert Team*, key verification and validation statements were addressed, confirming the framework's effectiveness in guiding auditors to obtain sufficient and reliable audit evidence for blockchain-based digital asset balances and transactions. Workshop feedback identified both strengths and areas for improvement, enhancing the framework's alignment with real-world audit practices. A key refinement involved addressing challenges in multi-signature setups, highlighting the framework's adaptability and the research's iterative approach.

The next chapter will illustrate and critically evaluate the framework's contributions to the audit profession and its relevance in the context of evolving blockchain technologies.

References

Baur, D. G., & Dimpfl, T. (2021). The volatility of Bitcoin and its role as a medium of exchange and a store of value. *Empirical Economics, 61*(5), 2663–2683.

Bo, X., & Wu, L. (2011). Earnings management information risk and audit opinion. *Audit Research, 1*, 90–97.

Hevner, A. R., March, S. T., & Park, J. (2004). Design science in information systems research. *MIS Quarterly, 28*(1), 75–105.

Meleschenko, S. S., Snetkova, T. A., Lyzhova, A. V., Markaryan, S. E., & Khafizova, L. V. (2020). Aspects of environmental issues in the audit evidence. *Procedia Environmental Science, Engineering and Management, 7*(3), 395–407.

Mullarkey, M. T., & Hevner, A. R. (2018). An elaborated action design research process model. *European Journal of Information Systems, 28*(1), 6–20.

Sein, M. K., Henfridsson, O., Purao, S., Rossi, M., & Lindgren, R. (2011). Action design research. *MIS Quarterly, 35*(1), 37–56.

Tian, J., & Xin, M. (2017). Literature review on audit opinion. *Journal of Modern Accounting and Auditing, 13*(6), 266–271.

CHAPTER 8

BTC_AF Demonstration

Abstract Chapter 8 transitions the development of the *Bitcoin Audit Framework* (BTC_AF) from theory to practical application. Through the Bitwise Bitcoin Spot ETF and Sixpence illustrations, the framework is tested across various bitcoin custody methods. Using the basic concepts from the ADR/eADR approach's observation-centric iteration, the BTC_AF is evaluated through authentic audit procedures, including address validation, transaction reconciliation, and cryptographic ownership testing.

This dual-case approach demonstrates the BTC_AF's robustness in addressing key audit assertions related to the *Statement of Financial Position* (SoFP) and *Statement of Profit or Loss* (SoPL). It accommodates technical complexities, such as *Hierarchical Deterministic* (HD) wallets, xpubs, multi-signature configurations, and transaction cut-offs. Each procedure reinforces the framework's relevance and adaptability to the challenges of blockchain auditing.

The BTC_AF demonstration confirms that it provides auditors with repeatable, verifiable procedures to obtain sufficient and reliable evidence in compliance with international standards. Iterative insights from these applications contribute to both refinement and the broader development of theory. This positions the BTC_AF as a scalable, practical tool that enhances audit assurance in the context of blockchain-based digital assets and an increasingly decentralized financial environment.

W. Olivier, P. Buys, *Auditing Bitcoin*,
https://doi.org/10.1007/978-981-95-5775-2_8

Keywords Audit assurance • Blockchain auditing • Digital assets • Cryptographic testing • Statement of financial position • Statement of profit or loss

JEL Classification M15 (IT Management): M42 (Auditing) • O31 (Innovation and Invention) • O33 (Technological Change)

8.1 Introduction

This chapter marks a critical phase in the *Bitcoin Audit Framework* (BTC_AF) development, shifting from the theoretical development and validation to a practical application demonstration. It demonstrates the framework's functionality and tests its ability to address the audit challenges of bitcoin-related balances and transactions. A dual approach is employed to illustrate the framework: publicly available data (Bitwise Bitcoin Spot ETF) demonstrates on-chain and real-world applicability, while a controlled, fictitious case (Sixpence) utilizes actual on-chain data, cryptography, and digital signatures to simulate scenarios involving sensitive or private information.

8.2 Applied Design-Science Principles

The observation-centric demonstration marks a key phase in evaluating the BTC_AF as the final artifact. Aligned with the iterative nature of the ADR/eADR methodology, this iteration focuses on observing the framework's real-world application to validate its effectiveness and identify potential areas for continuous improvement. This iteration embodies key design principles, specifically reciprocal shaping (principle 3), mutually influential roles (principle 4), and authentic and concurrent evaluation (principle 5), as per Mullarkey and Hevner (2018) and Sein et al. (2011). By analyzing outcomes from real-world applications, the demonstration aims to codify the integrated complexity (and requisite understanding) of the Bitcoin environment, strengthening the BTC_AF's theoretical foundation and practical utility.

8.3 Contextual BTC_AF Demonstration

The illustrated audit procedures address the technical and practical complexities of auditing in a digital asset environment, including blockchain mechanics, wallet configurations, multi-signature addresses, and xpubs. Two perspectives are applied as follows:

- To ensure practical relevance, the chapter combines publicly available data with controlled scenarios. Real-world data from the Bitwise Bitcoin Spot ETF, such as SEC filings, on-chain data and disclosed Bitcoin addresses, enables the transparent and verifiable application of several procedures. These can be reperformed using full Bitcoin nodes and tools specified in the BTC_AF.
- For procedures requiring sensitive or non-public data (e.g., ownership testing and multi-signature validation), a fictitious entity, Sixpence, is used. These scenarios replicate real audit conditions using real-world on-chain data, allowing auditors to reperform and validate procedures in a controlled environment.

This dual approach aims to offer comprehensive, practical guidance, confirming the BTC_AF's applicability and effectiveness in addressing the complexities of auditing Bitcoin-related balances and transactions.

8.3.1 General Information

The outcomes of the General Information-specific audit activities are presented in Tables 8.1, 8.2, and 8.3.

8.3.2 Statement of Financial Position

The outcomes of the SoFP-specific audit activities are presented in Tables 8.4, 8.5, 8.6, 8.7, 8.8, 8.9, 8.10, 8.11, 8.12, 8.13, 8.14, 8.15, 8.16, and 8.17.

8.3.3 Statement of Profit and Loss Procedures

The outcomes of the SoPL-specific audit activities are presented in Tables 8.18, 8.19, 8.20, 8.21, and 8.22.

8.4 Assessment of BTC_AF Demonstration

This observation-centric evolution iteration refines the BTC_AF through practical demonstration. Building on the earlier verification and validation iteration, the current iteration tests the framework's effectiveness using cases like Bitwise's self-custody model and Sixpence's hybrid wallet setup.

Aligned with key ADR/eADR principles, including reciprocal shaping, mutually influential roles, and authentic and concurrent evaluation, the demonstration ensures that the BTC_AF addresses real-world complexities auditors face when obtaining assurance over bitcoin-related balances and transactions. The BTC_AF demonstration incorporates insights from practice to maintain the framework's relevance and robustness across diverse custody arrangements and transaction types.

By integrating various wallet structures, i.e., single-signature, multi-signature, and HD wallets, and applying procedures like transaction reconciliation, cryptographic signing, and address derivation, the BTC_AF demonstrates its adaptability and assurance over key audit assertions.

This phase ensures the framework evolves to meet auditors' needs while contributing to a broader understanding of how to obtain reliable audit evidence for bitcoin-related balances and transactions. Through ongoing refinement, the observation-centric iteration further contributes to bridging theory and practice, confirming the BTC_AF as a scalable and dependable tool for navigating the evolving challenges of blockchain auditing.

Table 8.1 Procedure 1

Inquire whether management holds bitcoin through self-custody (on-chain), a third-party custodian, or a combination of both. • Bitwise uses segregated on-chain custody with keys managed by an intermediary. A simulated example included in procedure 5 will demonstrate third-party custody, illustrating how outsourced custody simplifies audit procedures and evidence requirements. • Sixpence practices self-custody, managing private keys directly. This requires auditors to address specific self-custody complexities, including ownership verification and control testing across varied wallet structures.

Table 8.2 Procedure 2

Inquire whether management uses a HD wallet structure to manage their bitcoin addresses. If so, obtain the wallet's xpub, associated addresses, and their derivation paths. Bitwise does not disclose details on HD wallet use, limiting verification through expubs and underscoring the sensitivity of such data and the audit challenges posed by private custody arrangements.

Sixpence uses an HD wallet to manage multiple bitcoin addresses, with extended keys for different types of addresses:

- **Legacy P2PKH (BIP 44) xpub**

xpub6BoFut8jRuVUS8nXMsqEbQ23N9JkC4xjGqow4RTu6eHjnboTJbEzaYGuV22i
ALyt1uM9a4CBscFcNyatgG7CWGRZSSFmMw4HVoMc53zKdAu

- **Nested Segwit P2SH-P2WPKH (BIP 49) ypub**

ypub6X8CKHJKDPtJMmu98yGpytVAHbXYtA8F1exuxiviKAH
zXGYcxJv1QjJyHDa3mhFFo7vycc2XDvo8XTne1Vbm67bEF7beXjBBLo1APig2W3Q

- **Native Segwit P2WPKH (BIP 84) zpub**

zpub6qkaCGsCqYQAFxnd9ZjbtWNyA997tQR3E6HAEkp3uTWt8
HpfHfgBwZGxhJKGAK36pUbvA9Vh9hNXbVyLv3Px6gAuEmSAEMZGG5fBjtkZko8

For replicability, these keys were derived from the BIP 32 root key (xprv9s21ZrQH143K2...) generated from the BIP 39 mnemonic phrase: *Cause melt glide bean turtle salute fancy rent rebuild beauty viable saddle*. This allows auditors to validate the linkage between mnemonic phrase, BIP 32 root key, xpub, and xpriv using an offline BIP39 tool. Refer to procedure 6 for the list of address types and derivation paths derived from the above extended keys.

Table 8.3 Procedure 3

Inquire with management about the blockchain cut-off date and time or block height used in their accounting policy for financial reporting (e.g., 31 December 2023, 23:59:59 UTC or block 823,785).

- Bitwise sets NAV cut-off at 30 Sep 2024, 8:00 p.m. ET (23:59:59 UTC), consistent with its accounting policy as set out in its SEC filings.
- Sixpence applies a year-end cut-off of 31 Dec 2024 at 23:59:59 UTC to capture all transactions for SoFP and SoPL testing.

Table 8.4 Procedure 4

Obtain management's schedule detailing nominal bitcoin balances per address and their functional currency values. Verify that the total functional currency balance aligns with the general ledger, trial balance, and financial statements.

Bitwise discloses its on-chain addresses but not the general ledger (GL) or trial balance (TB); reconciliation of the GL and TB to financial statements is therefore assumed. The address list omits individual nominal balances, but total holdings on 30 Sep 2024 serve as the reference point for validating aggregate balances.

Addresses

Addresses of Bitwise Bitcoin ETF: 30/09/2024			
1	bc1qhc8eryqvfk32llrtcd4meua04akunjj5dpdfvy	21	bc1qpdy0ymu9qyldv5axw5dur0t0x06sg965d5ztug
2	bc1qqejsnwmxswr3dpv6yuktjx7224wjt9yjng383c	22	bc1qlnltnmrezhwuuz78p7vdx2tsr9p6y66ez6p7hn
3	bc1qezsndnzeuxwaraeplr8dm30ml7gpgnm22xc0d8	23	bc1qetqgq0x4qf82tfge3awnh72xfcfgpxardkxnmh
4	bc1q9txxn6le0es4xr2nhdv6j49syrx6fcdjm887xj	24	bc1q2k5emamf5e4khwyl7nugnz3ra2tgaf6a3qur3e
5	bc1qkz6eqcul7l6kwjyyqhgueuj0e54yrplugkrm6a	25	bc1qltely8h429suzv04yacm379fdrl0e6yn59yyer
6	bc1qhhkef8vm8qfz6096v08hmfypwvly8p3azzh755	26	bc1qwhequaxm4ldk0kf6jy8clc2gnux9hjhrqn9zk2
7	bc1qgd2htxfflv32s9523esxh6cuenf80rjp38qtly	27	bc1q8k07yset47cxzmdz9sq3j4hjpv3m7eksxtteft
8	bc1qky4xywjl59d9ge83pjdhqs7ge8d3wtwgd5edm3	28	bc1q4qehlx90ec6v8wz4drcku8pmq688ykddp8t76w
9	bc1qf49cjsv7ajqmhj92zjzm4ynzsjj49us0p282au	29	bc1qgfcjpdcx88vwa48ufue54wnlyzawwq3h52fhla
10	bc1qlelqht9v90pkrev5w85lzdwvg8fluulqwsu30w	30	bc1qafqtvvkrus0mmpa377lfjua9u3jksczu28g745
11	bc1qcyfn2vlc8xxqrwgd5u3dy5cc7cqcpsqzmlydxu	31	bc1qej4cs4jasny3l369thx2qyjssam77rt8smvjqa
12	bc1qxaquc9l040mlk00prdykewvgg9ej0f6hlhw7x9	32	bc1qf70acnehlqr0hn0k97pvx25c6pluk5xh9jcvpt
13	bc1q7eem6f2unsp9s0nzgpfc50hmzugrv39a3h90rh	33	bc1q4p5sk0hqfcpl8gmcfvem0f270c880ndlsvldr9
14	bc1qhq9p9e6chat7jvkjjlffkl7ednkedue6c7r7z0	34	bc1ql2589wggx3wnsgx6frla5r2cnj6ysn8a8wmp5t
15	bc1q465da3ht56er2geskk0shrh9u8p84hyrx6nz2y	35	bc1q7s0pgkferccdud6zdxk5vt9tfu002dnd608t4p
16	bc1q2ky0v5pxjmd88rv2tpgszx5pqhynyyh3thqms5	36	bc1qc9rws3undptwdq7fslal089g36f48sendhthq4
17	bc1qgnhhcx7q3qn3n6u48u469hc833a6wgjwj07g0z	37	bc1q7s5da3aljvtz8j2dp7x9zdrhf9v0rn8wncqehk
18	bc1qgg22esucu0h8re0gtdas64nve60cyc8arawfvc	38	bc1qv9px59q0zdjwren7e39dg08gmlt7dmlmupks0r
19	bc1qlrt3vp77gt3r75lwfgm6qpy444jkazpjyzg4dc	39	bc1qv4pdepp9spsagp9h4vpvaa76c46gc2f9rryhg2
20	bc1qrlsen8frktrnmkjl2kvcprsrsrltfrrxzs58gv	40	bc1qz279nw7j400sz3vata2g9ys9y5lxprdxn7j96s

Bitwise Bitcoin ETF; Statements of Assets and Liabilities (September 30th, 2024)

Investment in bitcoin, at fair value (cost $2,068,421,000)	$2,502,767,000

Bitwise Bitcoin ETF: Schedule of Investments (September 30th, 2024)

	Quantity (BTC)	Cost	Fair value	Net Assets
Investment in BTC	39,435.5408	$2,068,421,000	$2,502,767,000	100.01%

While not strictly required, providing a detailed reconciliation between individual Bitcoin addresses and the financial statement balances would greatly simplify the verification process and enhance audit efficiency. Having a comprehensive list of nominal balances by address would allow auditors to directly investigate discrepancies, independently verify balances, minimize reliance on management, and ultimately strengthen the reliability of the audit.

Table 8.5 Procedure 5

For each address in management's schedule, use a transactional harvesting and aggregation tool to query a full Bitcoin node and confirm the nominal balance as of the financial reporting date and time

Uploaded the addresses from Table 8.4 into a reputable transactional harvesting and aggregation tool linked to a full Bitcoin node to retrieve transactional data up to 30 Sep 2024, 23:59:59 UTC. Compared the nominal balances to management's reported figures for accuracy. Any discrepancies were investigated with management; immaterial differences were recorded in the schedule of unadjusted audit differences.

Bitcoin queried addresses (September 30th, 2024)

	Bitcoin Addresses of Bitwise Bitcoin ETF	Nominal balance
1	bc1qhc8eryqvfk32llrtcd4meua04akunjj5dpdfvy	1,682.22
2	bc1qqejsnwmxswr3dpv6yuktjx7224wjt9yjng383c	1,000.00
3	bc1qezsndnzeuxwaraeplr8dm30ml7gpgnm22xc0d8	1,000.00
4	bc1q9txxn6le0es4xr2nhdv6j49syrx6fcdjm887xj	1,000.00
5	bc1qkz6eqcul7l6kwjyyqhgueuj0e54yrplugkrm6a	1,000.00
6	bc1qhhkef8vm8qfz6096v08hmfypwvly8p3azzh755	1,000.00
7	bc1qgd2htxfflv32s9523esxh6cuenf80rjp38qtly	1,000.00
8	bc1qky4xywjl59d9ge83pjdhqs7ge8d3wtwgd5edm3	1,000.00
9	bc1qf49cjsv7ajqmhj92zjzm4ynzsjj49us0p282au	1,000.00
10	bc1qlelqht9v90pkrev5w85lzdwvg8fluulqwsu30w	1,000.00
11	bc1qcyfn2vlc8xxqrwgd5u3dy5cc7cqcpsqzmlydxu	1,000.00
12	bc1qxaquc9l040mlk00prdykewvgg9ej0f6hlhw7x9	1,000.00
13	bc1q7eem6f2unsp9s0nzgpfc50hmzugrv39a3h90rh	1,000.00
14	bc1qhq9p9e6chat7jvkjjlffkl7ednkedue6c7r7z0	1,000.00
15	bc1q465da3ht56er2geskk0shrh9u8p84hyrx6nz2y	1,000.00
16	bc1q2ky0v5pxjmd88rv2tpgszx5pqhynyyh3thqms5	1,000.00
17	bc1qgnhhcx7q3qn3n6u48u469hc833a6wgjwj07g0z	1,000.00
18	bc1qgg22esucu0h8re0gtdas64nve60cyc8arawfvc	1,000.00
19	bc1qlrt3vp77gt3r75lwfgm6qpy444jkazpjyzg4dc	1,000.00
20	bc1qrlsen8frktrnmkjl2kvcprsrsrltfrrxzs58gv	1,000.00
21	bc1qpdy0ymu9qyldv5axw5dur0t0x06sg965d5ztug	1,000.00
22	bc1qlnltnmrezhwuuz78p7vdx2tsr9p6y66ez6p7hn	1,000.00
23	bc1qetqgq0x4qf82tfge3awnh72xfcfgpxardkxnmh	1,000.00
24	bc1q2k5emamf5e4khwyl7nugnz3ra2tgaf6a3qur3e	1,000.00
25	bc1qltely8h429suzv04yacm379fdrl0e6yn59yyer	1,000.00
26	bc1qwhequaxm4ldk0kf6jy8clc2gnux9hjhrqn9zk2	1,000.00
27	bc1q8k07yset47cxzmdz9sq3j4hjpv3m7eksxtteft	1,000.00
28	bc1q4qehlx90ec6v8wz4drcku8pmq688ykddp8t76w	1,000.00
29	bc1qgfcjpdcx88vwa48ufue54wnlyzawwq3h52fhla	1,000.00
30	bc1qafqtvvkrus0mmpa377lfjua9u3jksczu28g745	1,000.00
31	bc1qej4cs4jasny3l369thx2qyjssam77rt8smvjqa	1,000.00
32	bc1qf70acnehlqr0hn0k97pvx25c6pluk5xh9jcvpt	1,000.00
33	bc1q4p5sk0hqfcpl8gmcfvem0f270c880ndlsvldr9	1,000.00
34	bc1ql2589wggx3wnsgx6frla5r2cnj6ysn8a8wmp5t	1,000.00
35	bc1q7s0pgkferccdud6zdxk5vt9tfu002dnd608t4p	1,000.00
36	bc1qc9rws3undptwdq7fslal089g36f48sendhthq4	1,000.00
37	bc1q7s5da3aljvtz8j2dp7x9zdrhf9v0rn8wncqehk	1,000.00
38	bc1qv9px59q0zdjwren7e39dg08gmlt7dmlmupks0r	1,000.00
39	bc1qv4pdepp9spsagp9h4vpvaa76c46gc2f9rryhg2	900.00
40	bc1qz279nw7j400sz3vata2g9ys9y5lxprdxn7j96s	0.00
A	**Total**	**39,582.22**
B	**Balance as per financial statements (Table 8.4)**	**39,435.54**
A-B	**Difference (C)**	**146.68**
C/B	**Difference as a % of total bitcoin held**	**0.37%**
	USD Value of difference (0.37% x $2,502,767,000)	**$9,309,011**

- A discrepancy of 146.68 bitcoin was identified using the harvesting and aggregation tool versus Bitwise's reported balance. Lack of per-address balances prevents tracing to specific addresses, adding complexity.
- Discuss with management, assess materiality, and determine if inclusion in the schedule of unadjusted audit differences is required.

Table 8.5 (continued)

If a third-party custodian is used, the custodian's statement—including entity name, period-end, and nominal bitcoin balance—can be relied upon as sufficient evidence for existence, rights and obligations, valuation, and completeness. While further procedures are still needed for valuation and disclosure, third-party custody generally reduces audit effort and complexity compared to self-custody.

Simulated Example: 3rd Party Confirmation

Attention: Bitwise Bitcoin ETF

This letter confirms that Bitwise Bitcoin ETF maintains an individual trading account, 123456, with <Exchange EmmA>. This account was opened on 22 August 2022. The account summarizes the main account's asset balances, detailed below, as of 30 September 2024, 23:59:59 UTC, distinguished by available crypto-asset tokens in your spot wallets.

Overview

Date	User ID	Account Type	Wallet	Rate	Total Value	Spot Value
2024/09/30	123456	Main Account	Spot	1 BTC ≈ $63,464.76	39,435.5408 BTC	39,435.5408 BTC

Table 8.6 Procedure 6

If management uses an HD wallet structure, use the provided xpub and a BIP 32 deterministic key generator tool to derive child keys along the relevant derivation paths. Convert these keys into Bitcoin addresses using a pubkey-to-address conversion tool, then apply the transactional harvesting and aggregation tool to determine their nominal balances, as outlined in Procedure 5. Compare the resulting addresses with management's schedule to assess completeness.

Sixpence maintains HD and non-HD wallets. Using obtained xpubs, addresses were derived for Legacy (P2PKH), Nested SegWit (P2SH-P2WPKH), and Native SegWit (P2SH) via BIP 32 and pubkey-to-address tools, illustrated to depth 14. Actual structures may generate hundreds or thousands of addresses depending on business activity.

The BIP 32 root key supports additional address types. Derivation depth requested must align with the entity's business model.

Xpub, addresses, and derivation paths

	Address	Derivation path
	Legacy Address	
1	1H58PfYrW3rX1mYHtqRhE7JA7GvhUdpWqR	m/44'/0'/0'/0/0
2	1J28JUZURe2FiFxvyb3LzTA5reYFYDJt7R	m/44'/0'/0'/0/1
3	1JQ8TKNnUcf69AwtKx2TiqTj28GYHd7Ccj	m/44'/0'/0'/0/2
4	1AatQJxiV1tZ9RG48qphUgtLJ85D9bbBA3	m/44'/0'/0'/0/3
5	1KRWQUwWUUeUh6ifCUZ7q5pzY5w7U3E5U5	m/44'/0'/0'/0/4
6	1De4gH72yPpnNzKFCkjzTsXAHJSZxbR3pX	m/44'/0'/0'/0/5
7	1GDGTEYe33u8UM3yVWGny2oJyZ6Jb91tJs	m/44'/0'/0'/0/6
8	16JcVbjrrNRnq8zdtRU4XTNYLc35WwjMhA	m/44'/0'/0'/0/7
9	1P9SwL16f7mM4DDEWWhQJ7zePNk7tgdRh1	m/44'/0'/0'/0/8
10	1DXirmb98ZMBKYdKfiPSqkqmXcUwzjyTAj	m/44'/0'/0'/0/9
11	1AEQD5MsoQxu5fqJ5C4wx1rAmGtbZZmYNs	m/44'/0'/0'/0/10
12	1ELVzSvn17qU5FoAJvdNiFu1dT8QGFZ2Sr	m/44'/0'/0'/1/0
13	1AVsE8pK9mAfzwBzCtnhpANEYJpLxafWSS	m/44'/0'/0'/1/1
14	19ZwYnGq3Y6xjjAKmwcf34DdbcjdKcSE3Y	m/44'/0'/0'/1/2
	Nested Segwit P2SH - P2WPKH	
1	3LzbyP9nZSjJyjCEyqBSCbfpjdxibTvFf8	m/49'/0'/0'/0/0
2	39ZEALzwezoWzS1owTrN6JaE8LA5HXRk7Q	m/49'/0'/0'/0/1
3	36ZBwEQNtmqAfoXCqYwhr3Qvu8d477SxbC	m/49'/0'/0'/0/2
4	3JQqAcr2GKaQnH71XF7aEcsRYQJP6RRQY9	m/49'/0'/0'/0/3
5	3ButtfcSt2oZ2EHthLuDuh86kmqzv4nYKh	m/49'/0'/0'/0/4
6	38xYpgUribzbWG8eK2vMsnvYNcvrTU951R	m/49'/0'/0'/0/5
7	37jBRNo2hbC6w9J8HYsrRiteyXseRsdH8U	m/49'/0'/0'/0/6
8	383ZM6zLjSVafTcyG3ee8FVk7ZSjMdmWWf	m/49'/0'/0'/0/7
9	33NBDTHWLJm7x4U4YVj2uM3yL3bx5khr3P	m/49'/0'/0'/0/8
10	3ACY8DYgbsEUarZT5kveAybrRBJrQdANkP	m/49'/0'/0'/0/9
11	3Ld27YZjj2BRq8yPggnVm93bBKKFPtWyyj	m/49'/0'/0'/0/10
12	3JS4XDbZWQVqQEeqo9FWH9Qidizw14oAZh	m/49'/0'/0'/1/0
13	3DCYzpv8WgGwv3En9rMaPpTPub89VqajuY	m/49'/0'/0'/1/1
14	3CipvtRAbwwAdGL7BAecaCfB7EzMZUeHtT	m/49'/0'/0'/1/2
	Native Segwit P2SH	
1	bc1qe6z54p3tvda5kdstx0p8xnhp5p0jr8d4glt0qf	m/84'/0'/0'/0/0
2	bc1qkd2fp493l46wg7rfmuj672f03zh6czcrkdk39l	m/84'/0'/0'/0/1
3	bc1qf8sr0gdw3zgdpaykmtqwc9sryjg5av2ku6p2kl	m/84'/0'/0'/0/2
4	bc1q2tnw60uccuhd9pwv0u29l5ttdggkzzl0lnystm	m/84'/0'/0'/0/3
5	bc1qvkk0ldsu9pnlxx3rwcrutcz0f8zy2gepqpww92	m/84'/0'/0'/0/4
6	bc1qylcylrtv73ska7xk649p22k7x24jevcecxtucy	m/84'/0'/0'/0/5
7	bc1q7z0d0q0y5dn9254yxsthqf6dcw64cps4lkdsu5	m/84'/0'/0'/0/6
8	bc1qnkxgvun7ve6ksg5c7kx2hrzgy7ncwrxjkmmp5h	m/84'/0'/0'/0/7
9	bc1qkmuxq5pn5pf4mq0u9srhhhzl94kt6ypu5gm5ym	m/84'/0'/0'/0/8
10	bc1qqmyr5c5l2k4dtu388t8z0rqg3hwv4jc0mzzzy2	m/84'/0'/0'/0/9
11	bc1qlcd5dz3hmn4h39r4r764q2grxx9w5t2jk0tpnv	m/84'/0'/0'/0/10
12	bc1qdq90yl6dw34zksx5h5075q5452gxtpvsxf2wpz	m/84'/0'/0'/1/0
13	bc1qpufvcs4p43ana5xh9yc2ktwkje68mmqah56e4s	m/84'/0'/0'/1/1
14	bc1q6t3bc1q5fmthqnwr84rfdla6aar7el5t37dx86fm7pucn	m/84'/0'/0'/1/2

Used the transaction harvesting and aggregation tool (see Procedure 5) to retrieve balances as at year-end. All addresses showed zero balances except for the following:

Table 8.6 (continued)

Sixpence Bitcoin Balances (December 31st, 2024)

	Address	Balance
1	1KRWQUwWUUeUh6ifCUZ7q5pzY5w7U3E5U5	0.00002500
2	16JcVbjrrNRnq8zdtRU4XTNYLc35WwjMhA	0.00001644
3	19ZwYnGq3Y6xjjAKmwcf34DdbcjdKcSE3Y	0.00001699
4	3JQqAcr2GKaQnH71XF7aEcsRYQJP6RRQY9	0.00001919
5	bc1qkmuxq5pn5pf4mq0u9srhhhzl94kt6ypu5gm5ym	0.00002138
6	1ELVzSvn17qU5FoAJvdNiFu1dT8QGFZ2Sr	0.00001101
7	1KRWQUwWUUeUh6ifCUZ7q5pzY5w7U3E5U5	0.00002500

As of 31 Dec 2024, 23:59:59 UTC, certain addresses held UTXOs. The list requested in Procedure 2 and included in the bottom of Table 8.7 revealed that address 19ZwYnGq3Y6xjjAKmwcf34DdbcjdKcSE3Y—derived from the xpub—was missing from management's submission. This indicates a completeness issue, as not all UTXO-holding addresses under the entity's control were reported. Follow up with management to determine the reason and address in line with audit methodology.

Table 8.7 Procedure 7

If management uses a hybrid custodian, such as a cryptocurrency exchange, to convert bitcoin to fiat, other digital assets or vice versa, obtain the entity's transaction history from the hybrid custodian for the relevant financial period. Identify all send/receive transactions involving the hybrid custodian and other Bitcoin addresses and inquire about any unidentified addresses to detect potential omissions from management's provided list of bitcoin addresses and balances.

Sixpence uses a cryptocurrency exchange for bitcoin-to-fiat conversions. Management provided a transaction report for the year ended 31 Dec 2024 and a list of related on-chain addresses. Verification of the accuracy and completeness of these reports is necessary but falls outside the current scope of the BTC_AF.

Hybrid custodian list of transactions

Timestamp (UTC)	Description	Transaction ID	Currency	Value	Notes
13/01/2024 12:45	Buy Bitcoin using USD	N/A	BTC	1.5753	1
28/01/2024 03:05	Sent Bitcoin to bc1qjstnlfrwsljxvvxy5uu75w2fxpjfgsz6rn9zgp	ed6926ed43d5d7433415cc16daba3dca889d9256ecfe6fd9e0ae2e744ad8a0aa	BTC	0.0007	2
28/01/2024 06:56	Received Bitcoin from 1GbhH6bHivu41Eun3ST4qRvVQTAd8Dcoyd	98953dbd8e3325a3d3446c94acc4cbdb5f6998947c2fc57a0a1f06550c0d8e7b	BTC	0.11672519	3
05/04/2024 03:23	Sent Bitcoin to 15zoEBoPixC39YHQV562LZc7woTdmE3itz	ee408a61da0f02f394fc1cd212f54bb4a9ff2a1e71545a1885a09df05666531e	BTC	0.5	4
01/05/2024 05:21	Sell Bitcoin to USD	N/A	BTC	0.05241	5
14/06/2024 01:41	Sent Bitcoin to bc1qfpc6ugxgd2vgwt3xmtp7z359y870rfk8ft6032	e79fb9eb2ef7329388d9302ef6e22b64d3514921af7287a434ae21a46490d729	BTC	0.02243125	6
21/06/2024 03:12	Sent Bitcoin to bc1q59med76qadc7jsstz0ck29ykn8luzhde6v8yya	c829ea1aedc54be7ee3fed901fe37026bd97a2a6bc23d07ba0ac9b857ecde9ef	BTC	0.01129698	7
12/06/2024 09:21	Received Bitcoin from bc1qph43qgsz293whtawrxjyde7sw0u0sq7h72ctfa	952cdfdb2aa844d5de85b87cdb32e50241546c1eccccaade315256a99610b42e	BTC	0.00440908	8
25/07/2024 03:36	Received Bitcoin from 12Rw6UjCPPBBsGCDSuzGJz1ejcp6f47Mhf	ad2c7d4c293aad2a08acc1d985e9e3aac43bf9c0845b3691c0fc89b749bca944	BTC	0.6924	9
05/12/2024 03:23	Sent Bitcoin to 3ChCFSzS9quhHrfWgLJkazqGz2qktqXZi4	f0823a09ce7dba55d4e8706f6f86127dab77446217d40bca7c924555261f2516	BTC	0.27649825	10

- **Note 1 & 5:** Transactions involving bitcoin purchases or sales on the exchange and are not relevant to this procedure.
- **Notes 2, 3, 7, 9 & 10:** The Bitcoin addresses are included in management's list (Table 8.8), supporting the completeness of the address list.
- **Notes 4 & 6:** The Bitcoin addresses are not on management's list. The auditor must inquire about the recipients and, if payments are claimed to external parties, obtain supporting documentation.
- **Note 8:** The sending address is not on management's list. If management states it is from a customer or third party, supporting documentation should be obtained to verify the claim.

Table 8.8 Procedure 8

Using management's schedule of Bitcoin addresses and balances, reconciled with the trial balance and financial statements, recalculate the functional currency values based on the spot price of bitcoin and the applicable accounting policy at period-end.

Using Bitwise as an example, Table 8.4 shows that at 30 September 2024, 23:59:59 UTC, 39,435.5408 bitcoin was valued at $2,502,767,000. As Bitwise applies fair value accounting, the auditor should compare this amount with the CoinMarketCap spot price at cut-off to confirm accuracy. A regulated pricing source could also potentially be utilized.

BTC/USD spot price (September 30th, 2024)

Open	High	Low	Close	Volume	Timestamp
65,634.66	65,635.05	59,878.8	62,818.95	221,870,167,579	2024-09-30T00:00:00

Based on CoinMarketCap, bitcoin's closing value at cut-off on 30 September 2024, was $62,818.95 with $221.87 billion in daily trading volume, confirming high liquidity. The one-second variance from the cut-off is immaterial. This spot price is applied to the nominal balance to verify the reported functional currency value.

Valuation consideration

Variance calculation		
A	Value of bitcoin per CoinMarketCap	62,818.95
B	Nominal amount of bitcoin held per financial statements	39,435.5408
A x B	USD value (C)	2,477,299,215
D	USD value as per financial statements	2,502,767,000
D-C	Difference	25,467,785
	Variance in %	1.02%

Applying the CoinMarketCap USD/BTC spot price to the nominal balance shows a $25,467,758 (1.02%) variance from Bitwise's 30 September 2024 reported value. The auditor must assess materiality under the accounting framework and audit methodology—investigating with management if material, or recording as an unadjusted difference if immaterial.
Under IFRS, if bitcoin is classified as an intangible asset, impairment is tested by comparing cost ($2,068,421,000) to market value ($2,477,299,215). As market value exceeds cost, no impairment arises. However, impairment would need evaluation if prices fall below $63,464.76 per BTC.

Table 8.9 Procedure 9

Inquire whether management's bitcoin addresses are single-signature or multi-signature. For ownership testing across multi-signature, single-signature, and HD wallets, sixpence is used as a reference example due to the lack of detailed ownership data for bitwise. Sixpence's diverse custody arrangements—Spanning single-signature, multi-signature, and HD wallets—Provide an ideal basis to illustrate audit procedures for verifying control and ownership, including testing private keys or signing thresholds for multi-signature wallets, validating single-signature ownership via cryptographic message signing or transaction execution, and addressing the complexities of HD wallets and xpubs.

Table 8.10 Procedure 10

Inquire whether management can perform cryptographic message signing on their single- or multi-signature addresses.
Sixpence can sign messages for both wallet types, but ownership verification will also include a movement of funds demonstration.

Table 8.11 Procedure 11

Provide management with a unique phrase containing numbers, letters, and symbols. Request they sign it with the private key of the address under test (per their schedule) and submit the signature to the audit team for validation under procedure 12.
For illustration, address 19mNo9zFTnanF8XHAJLZeX6MpMuQXhh6XD (Table 8.7) is used for ownership testing via cryptographic message signing. Sample size selection depends on audit methodology, materiality, and risk, and may be expanded to include xpub-related coverage.

To enable re-performance, the associated private key (KxnD7krRXzio5ah3uGC6xaqukfVUw8sxD412mU3qzHchTeHN8JoV) is disclosed. The test message *ownership//ControL.Test-2008* is simplified and will produce signature *H++M3pQGMm1QNh9OTD0M093aqT/TBc/WAiqzte95NYK7TOe5bVUfALIVsA94Nhe+3mMYBd/1cIxk2snQJjcVUW4=*; however, the second researcher-practitioner team recommends including the entity name, purpose, block hash, and date for stronger security and uniqueness.
Example enhanced message:
"Silver Sixpence confirms ownership of 19mNo9zFTnanF8XHAJLZeX6MpMuQXhh6XD on 5 January 2024 with block height 877,944 and hash 0000000000000000001087f693daab272e3c0d05ceb9a295c3e12d3a9a43a11"
produced the verifiable signature (however, this will not be used for the example below):
IPWIZVydXZQR6m4hcm/qvu2DdR511s1kBWvrB4MuwmLFdfnjDrFZkECWFSmKDjQvqHbZELVzGdLlvZR9yC1xAcg=
Management is unlikely to use open-source tools for cryptographic message signing due to private key security concerns, and may instead use their own preferred methods. Regardless of the tool chosen, as long as it implements the bitcoin protocol's deterministic digital signature algorithms, the resulting signature will be consistent and verifiable.
Cryptographic signature

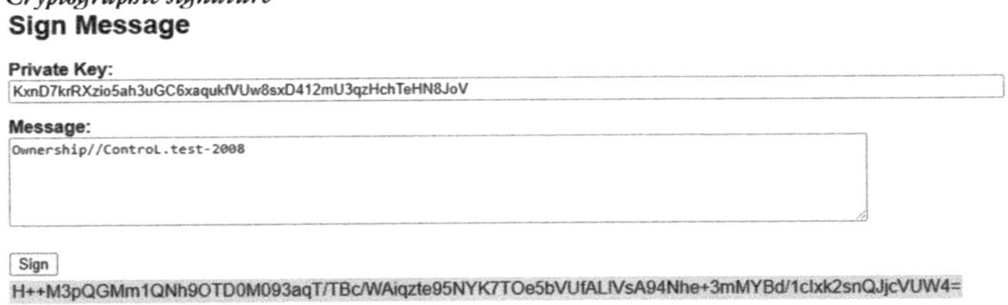

The signature produced *H++M3pQGMm1QNh9OTD0M093aqT/TBc/WAiqzte95NYK7TOe5bVUfALIVsA94Nhe+3mMYBd/1cIxk2snQJjc VUW4=*, which can be used to cryptographically verify knowledge of the private key and therefore ownership, as illustrated in procedure 12.

Table 8.12 Procedure 12

Use a cryptographic message verification tool to validate the signature provided by management. Input the address being tested, the unique message, and the cryptographic signature, obtained in procedure 11, into the tool.

Using the verification tool, the following information was entered and validated:

- Address

19mNo9zFTnanF8XHAJLZeX6MpMuQXhh6XD

- Message

Ownership//ControL.Test-2008

- Signature: *H++M3pQGMm1QNh9OTD0M093aqT/TBc/WAiqzte95NYK7TOe5bV UfALIVsA94Nhe+3mMYBd/1cIxk2snQJjcVUW4=*

Cryptographic message signing input

(*continued*)

Table 8.12 (continued)

Cryptographic message validation

Validating the cryptographic signature confirms that the private key was used to sign the message, providing sufficient evidence that management controls the address and owns the associated UTXO

Table 8.13 Procedure 13

If management cannot perform cryptographic message signing, request them to sweep the entire balance from the address in question to another address they control and provide the transaction hash.

The target address bc1q44ueff4d7yp487kwqstmzt78865pzk3gqzcpkg (Table 8.7) held 0.00006048 BTC. On 22 October 2024 at 19:30 UTC, on request, management transferred the full balance to bc1qeq2m259rlh0marmqdlfddlnfxeddt4l4z4ne3d. The provided transaction hash, b4547fa24b8bb4ad954e3f6c439cc21bc599e26538fc3f6387f508c9a71c5a42, was verified via a full-node explorer, confirming source, destination, amount, and timestamp. This successful transfer offers strong evidence of management's control of the private key and the address.

Transaction confirmation

BLOCKCHAIN	BITCOIN
TRANSACTION ID	b4547fa24b8bb4ad954e3f6c439cc21bc599e26538fc3f6387f508c9a71c5a42
DATE & TIME	Oct 22, 2024 · 19:30 (UTC)
TRANSACTION STATUS	In block 866,886 · CONFIRMED ✓
TRANSACTION FEE	0.00004032 BTC · 2.72 USD

SENDERS (INPUTS):

#	Address Id	Amount
1	bc1q44ueff4d7yp487kwqstmzt78865pzk3gqzcpkg	- 0.00006048 BTC 4.08 USD

RECIPIENTS (OUTPUTS):

#	Address Id	Amount
1	bc1qeq2m259rlh0marmqdlfddlnfxeddt4l4z4ne3d	+ 0.00002016 BTC 1.36 USD

Table 8.14 Procedure 14

If management's list includes multi-signature addresses, obtain the m-of-n configuration for each multi-signature address as well as the corresponding "m" public keys required to authorize transactions for each of these addresses.

Included in sixpence's controlled addresses is a single multi-signature address, 34tWazF2HX8XXpWceFECCTYuK6X7Z78aJw, used for this and the following procedure. Management confirmed it is a 2-of-3 P2SH address, requiring two of three authorized public keys to sign a transaction, and provided all three public keys in hexadecimal format for reference in the procedures.

- *023e43ea1ec0dde69c8b9cad77abe2c307c3bda82e6cd1a7d692947a122c10a0f6*
- *02963c5a38cf67f24d837db75fa57a10aaba68cffb3d02f9c8a779ff465f527c99*
- *030061a60dcac921a54c283bd1928404b9deafecf53b4ee35e8314d20602278718*

Table 8.15 Procedure 15

For each multi-signature address in management's list, use a blockchain explorer linked to a full node to locate an output transaction that reveals the m-of-n signature setup. Retrieve the P2SH redeem script from the transaction and compare it with the configuration provided by management. Convert each of the "m" public keys into bitcoin addresses using a pubkey-to-address tool and perform ownership testing as outlined in procedures 11 and/or 13.

The identified P2SH multi-signature address was queried via a full-node explorer. Transaction ID 66b913219ee4d11086eda36970acf4be94068ea5c6a74d71943126e271bf1990 revealed the redeem script, confirming a 2-of-3 setup.

OP_PUSHNUM_2
OP_PUSHBYTES_33
023e43ea1ec0dde69c8b9cad77abe2c307c3bda82e6cd1a7d692947a122c10a0f6
OP_PUSHBYTES_33
02963c5a38cf67f24d837db75fa57a10aaba68cffb3d02f9c8a779ff465f527c99
OP_PUSHBYTES_33
030061a60dcac921a54c283bd1928404b9deafecf53b4ee35e8314d20602278718
OP_PUSHNUM_3
OP_CHECKMULTISIG

The extracted P2SH redeem script confirms a 2-of-3 multi-signature setup (OP_PUSHNUM_2 and OP_PUSHNUM_3). The three hex-format public keys can be converted into bitcoin address types (e.g., legacy PUBKEY, P2PKH, P2SH_P2WPKH) using a key-to-address conversion tool a shown below.

Table 8.15 (continued)

Public key to address conversion tool

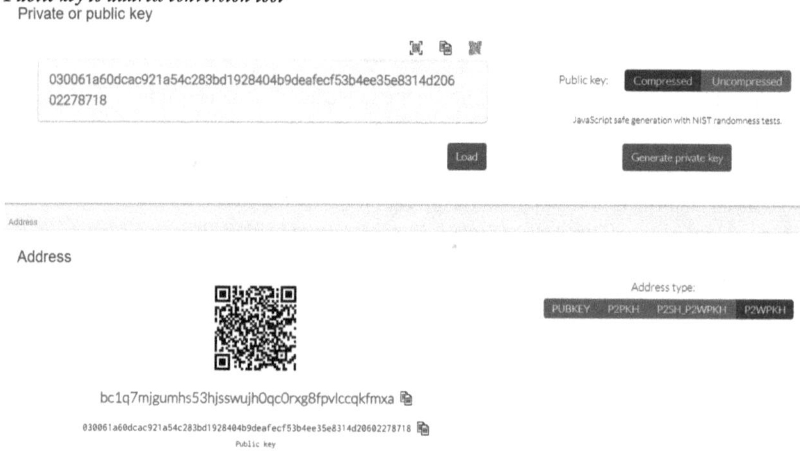

When management provides cryptographic proof for the required 2-of-3 public keys, they may first convert these keys into a specific bitcoin address type before signing. The auditor must understand which address type was used, as this affects how ownership and control are verified. If there is no transaction revealing the redeem script, the auditor can request management to execute a transaction from the multi-signature address to expose it. If that's not feasible, management should provide the details of the multi-signature setup, which can then be used with a locking script-to-address tool to recreate and verify the address and public keys. The P2SH and P2WSH script examples assume a 2-of-3 setup but can be adjusted as needed to match the actual configuration.

OP_PUSHNUM_2
OP_PUSHBYTES_33
<Public key 1>
OP_PUSHBYTES_33
<Public key 2>
OP_PUSHBYTES_33
<Public key 3>
OP_PUSHNUM_3
OP_CHECKMULTISIG

OP_PUSHNUM_2: Indicates that at least two signatures are required to satisfy the multi-signature setup.
OP_PUSHBYTES_33 <Public key 1>: Pushes the first 33-byte public key onto the stack.
OP_PUSHBYTES_33 <Public key 2>: Pushes the second 33-byte public key onto the stack.
OP_PUSHBYTES_33 <Public key 3>: Pushes the third 33-byte public key onto the stack.
OP_PUSHNUM_3: Indicates a total of 3 public keys in the multi-signature setup.
OP_CHECKMULTISIG: Executes the multi-signature verification, checking whether at least two valid signatures (out of the three possible public keys) are provided.

Table 8.16 Procedure 16

If the entity uses an HD wallet structure with multiple addresses derived from a single xpub, the auditor can test ownership of one associated address, i.e., the target address, to verify control over the entire structure. Using the xpub, the target address, and its derivation path, apply a BIP 32 deterministic key generator and pubkey-to-address tool to reproduce the target address, confirming its link to the xpub.
Sixpence provided extended keys (procedure 2) derived from its BIP 32 root key, enabling the generation of child and grandchild keys for different bitcoin address types (see procedure 6). A BIP 32 tool can confirm if an address is derived from the xpub, proving linkage and control without exposing the xpriv.
In this example, target address 1H58PfYrW3rX1mYHtqRhE7JA7GvhUdpWqR was tested. Management signed *ownership//ControL.Test-2008*, producing signature *ICruxPNjWJuJhuS48Y8WSPJR740LPTsJK3fvNAh+uCChJCp95rEoJetz+608CrtHG/FU+1+dZqV4gM87BRkTdtY=*, which was verified (procedure 12).
Using xpub *xpub6BoFut8jRuVUS8nXMsqEbQ23N9JkC4xjGqow4RTu6eHjnboTJbEzaYGuV22iALyt1uM9a4CBscFcNyatgG7CWGRZSSFmMw4HVoMc53zKdAu* and derivation path *m/44'/0'/0'/0/1*, the derived child key matched the target address, confirming linkage to the xpub and management's control.
This verification demonstrates knowledge of the xpriv and control of all derived keys. Ownership testing should be performed for each xpub type, as each has a unique derivation path and child xprivs.

Table 8.17 Procedure 17

The auditor must ensure that the entity's bitcoin holdings are appropriately accounted for and disclosed by its accounting policy and the applicable financial reporting framework. Assessing bitcoin presentation and disclosure requirements is outside the BTC_AF's scope, as disclosures depend on entity-specific factors.

Table 8.18 Procedure 18

Ask management if the schedule includes empty (spent) addresses that held UTXOs during the period. If not, request an updated list or derive all linked addresses from the xpub and test ownership per procedures 11, 13, and/or 17.
For Sixpence, management's schedule lists all addresses with current or past UTXOs as of 31 December 2024. The auditor also derived related addresses from the xpub to verify completeness. However, one address was missing (see Procedure 6), indicating a potential completeness issue requiring follow-up.

Table 8.19 Procedure 19

Use the transaction harvesting and aggregation tool to retrieve all bitcoin transactions linked to the addresses in management's updated schedule and/or the xpub for the financial period.

From Procedure 19 onward, Sixpence is assumed to use two Bitcoin addresses for payments and receipts:

- bc1q44ueff4d7yp487kwqstmzt78865pzk3gqzcpkg
- bc1qeq2m259rlh0marmqdlfddlnfxeddt4l4z4ne3d

Transaction listing

TX ID	Timestamp (UTC)	Increase	Decrease
8926bc47c0c33fa3b0303cf49eb094b2d39952e24cdae56e8d48ffb3b4b129d9	2024-10-24T15:27:25		572.3394816
1357fe1706aa16a64ab30f96c482a08c93b5b219558c7fab883fd766491cfb17	2024-10-22T19:50:05	0.00004032	
27c1d43d8f995c3c461fa152178546cfed8227ac0aa9bfd501d75e39637f6798	2024-10-22T19:50:05	0.00004032	
a2b3c60262edde7149390931d9001d71393c5f80c1c7786960d8450cb7d16595	2024-10-22T19:50:05	0.00010245	
b4547fa24b8bb4ad954e3f6c439cc21bc599e26538fc3f6387f508c9a71c5a42	2024-10-22T19:30:42		0.00006048
163e6fa49293d4e3e23b121d4fdc216bfe1ddeb5b385cc19a465a2f0f45b47ba	2024-10-22T19:30:42	0.00014800	
b4547fa24b8bb4ad954e3f6c439cc21bc599e26538fc3f6387f508c9a71c5a42	2024-10-22T19:30:42	0.00002016	
5095d398ca17c4496b5fbb7528ca05cd71bff4d78952db291dadf96046b83813	2024-10-22T19:06:46	0.00007704	
22516266e71d630ba2f32180a29b6558a0fa0ed1eb70917b4b202cfe5a03a614	2024-10-22T18:21:25	572.3390533	
19a124ce8e7d14d463ad2b2ddb6ac5d343f33a304375aed7ce3710136b1e8372	2024-05-08T17:07:45		592.3239448
71ce6df7df6758773a844ea14568427602da89b861b00b363082db3b1f0b2792	2024-05-08T17:07:45	0.00006048	
788f37ddeca0218e6f92eb039183ef98021bfb02682857026630a74aca22d995	2024-05-08T16:16:23	0.00093952	
03dda35999fc8478e1544ac38603542b04371b5d039d42db1b8d61fae5556050	2024-05-07T14:10:44	0.00006300	
4ac6138c5fbfd3c48a8309d6d9f380054b6294f037ebd2fa58ec810e967cdbd7	2024-05-07T14:02:51	32.70676422	
18d3a8c63d0ae64944738f612c42b86f870e1522c789390b0afe11cf3e7612de	2024-05-06T14:10:30	0.00007560	
d512347c482a55993afde31854fba4c60a75c0b2572866487de8935ffd1505b2	2024-05-06T13:42:17	389.6641179	
0050eee0d7e5f9ac80d6cb2b72dff97693c8de3d342de6645dde8748be9483b0	2024-05-06T10:47:09	0.00015187	
5588eeb60f040b14a0975664d0cb1dfdcf67e9c93eb9a751b0f9efe1000a5e8b	2024-05-06T10:41:27	149.9998481	
4165e2dc2771e58ff5891329c5615aa47bbbff76df969c6b9d337ad7a4f5d29c	2024-05-02T15:49:24	0.00011556	
0ae5b8aa1700960d47af736cbaa964200d766580571e600ffb874713cc968ff8	2024-05-02T15:09:23	19.95186905	

Table 8.20 Procedure 20

Inquire with management about which general ledger or trial balance accounts were used for recording the sending or receiving of bitcoin-related payments.

Sixpence records bitcoin transactions in two ledger accounts:

- 1000/000 – Revenue in bitcoin
- 6000/000 – Expenses in bitcoin

Revenue general ledger

Description	Txn ID	Date	Delta	BTC USD Spot	USD Value
Customer A	1357fe1706	22/10/2024	0.000040	$66,871.26	$2.70
Customer B	27c1d43d8f	22/10/2024	0.000040	$66,871.26	$2.70
Customer C	a2b3c60262	22/10/2024	0.000102	$66,871.26	$6.85
Customer B	163e6fa492	22/10/2024	0.000148	$66,873.32	$9.90
Customer B	b4547fa24b	22/10/2024	0.000020	$66,873.32	$1.35
Customer G	5095d398ca	22/10/2024	0.000077	$66,875.85	$5.15
Customer A	22516266e7	22/10/2024	572.33905	$66,880.66	$38,278,411.28
Customer B	71ce6df7df	08/05/2024	0.000060	$62,523.15	$ 3.78
Customer D	788f37ddec	08/05/2024	0.000940	$62,245.25	$ 58.48
Donation	03dda35999	07/05/2024	0.000063	$63,282.11	$3.99
Customer X	4ac6138c5f	07/05/2024	32.706764	$63,397.42	$2,073,524.34
Customer E	18d3a8c63d	06/05/2024	0.000076	$63,970.48	$ 4.84
Customer Q	d512347c48	06/05/2024	389.66411	$63,968.84	$24,926,360.40
Customer F	0050eee0d7	06/05/2024	0.000152	$64,166.29	$9.74
Customer F	5588eeb60f	06/05/2024	149.99984	$64,263.11	$9,639,456.82
Customer G	4165e2dc27	02/05/2024	0.000116	$59,233.10	$6.84
Customer W	Dne3n32jj22	02/05/2024	1.00215	$59,221.13	$59,348.55
Customer A	0ae5b8aa17	02/05/2024	19.951869	$59,221.13	$ 1,181,572.30

Expense general ledger

Description	Txn ID	Date	Delta	BTC USD Spot	USD Value
Supplier A	8926bc47c0	24/10/2024	572.34	$67,686.63	$ 38,739,731.90
Supplier B	b4547fa24b	22/10/2024	0.000060	$66,873.32	$ 4.04

Sixpence's ERP links the first 10 digits of each Bitcoin transaction ID to the transaction amount and related ledger entry, improving tracking and on-chain reconciliation. It also records the spot price at the transaction time, ensuring accurate reporting.

Table 8.21 Procedure 21

For each bitcoin-associated account identified in procedure 20, reconcile the complete transaction listing (or sample) with transactions from the addresses in management's schedule used for sending or receiving bitcoin. Sixpence uses two bitcoin-linked accounts, 1000/000 (revenue) and 6000/000 (expenses), associated with addresses: • bc1q44ueff4d7yp487kwqstmzt78865pzk3gqzcpkg • bc1qeq2m259rlh0marmqdlfddlnfxeddt4l4z4ne3d. All transactions from Jan 1–Dec 31, 2024, were retrieved via a harvesting tool and fully reconciled with the general ledger due to low volume. • Unrecorded on blockchain: Revenue entry of 1.00215 BTC (ID Dne3n32jj22, 2 Apr 2024) in ledger only—possible fictitious entry or undisclosed address. • Omission from ledger: On-chain transaction of 592.32 BTC (ID 19a124ce8e7…, 8 Apr 2025) absent from ledger—requires urgent follow-up due to material value. The reconciliation also validated the cut-off using blockchain timestamps. No further discrepancies noted for the period.

8.5 Summary

This chapter demonstrated the BTC_AF's practical effectiveness in addressing the complexities of auditing bitcoin-related balances and transactions. Through real-world and illustrative scenarios involving Bitwise and Sixpence, the framework proved robust across various wallet types, custody models, and audit procedures. It effectively supports auditors in validating key SoFP and SoPL assertions, ensuring compliance with international auditing requirements. The reflection highlights the BTC_AF's adaptability and relevance, reinforced by its iterative development through the applied design approach. This ensures the framework remains aligned with the evolving demands of auditing bitcoin-associated balances and transactions.

The next chapter will build on these findings, summarizing contributions, acknowledging limitations, and outlining future research opportunities.

Table 8.22 Procedure 22

Use the transaction harvesting and aggregation tool to obtain all bitcoin transactions linked to the addresses in management's schedule for the financial period. Reconcile these, either entirely or on a sample basis, by converting the nominal bitcoin amounts to the functional currency using the applicable spot rate. Compare the converted values to related income and expense entries in the general ledger to ensure accurate SoPL reporting following the entity's accounting policy and framework.

Management provided the general ledger with nominal bitcoin values and spot rates. Transactional data from the Bitcoin addresses was previously reconciled for occurrence, completeness, and cut-off. To test functional currency accuracy, a sample of two revenue items and one expense item is selected. Bitcoin amounts (column delta) are converted using the applicable USD/BTC spot rate from CoinMarketCap to verify recorded fiat values.

Revenue samples for accuracy

Sample	#1	#2
Txn ID	22516266e7	788f37ddec
Date	22/10/2024	08/05/2024
Delta (A)	572.339053	0.000940
BTC USD Spot	$66,880.66	$62,245.25
USD Value (D)	$38,278,411.28	$58.48
CoinMarketCap BTC/USD Spot (B)	$66,929.30	$61,448.39
Recalculated difference (A x B)	$38,306,251.51	$57.73
Diff (D- (A x B))	$-27,840.23	$0.75
Total difference in USD		**$-27,839.48**
Difference as a %		**0.07%**

Expenses sample for accuracy

Sample	#1
Txn ID	8926bc47c0
Date	24/10/2024
Delta (A)	572.34
BTC USD Spot	$67,686.63
USD Value (D)	$38,739,731.90
CoinMarketCap BTC/USD Spot (B)	$67,741.12
Recalculated difference (A x B)	$38,770,914.92
Diff (D- (A x B))	$-31,183.03
Total difference in USD	**$-31,183.03**
Difference as a %	**0.08%**

The samples tested revealed minor differences, which should be evaluated for reasonableness against the applicable accounting framework and engagement-specific materiality thresholds. Given their insignificance relative to the total ledger balance, the auditor may deem them acceptable, clearly trivial, or choose to extrapolate them to assess the potential overall impact.

References

Mullarkey, M. T., & Hevner, A. R. (2018). An elaborated action design research process model. *European Journal of Information Systems, 28*(1), 6–20.
Sein, M. K., Henfridsson, O., Purao, S., Rossi, M., & Lindgren, R. (2011). Action design research. *MIS Quarterly, 35*(1), 37–56.

CHAPTER 9

Concluding Discussion

Abstract A critical challenge in the contemporary audit profession is obtaining sufficient and reliable audit evidence for digital asset-related balances and transactions. In response to this growing need, this book elucidates the development of the *Bitcoin Audit Framework* (BTC_AF), a structured and practical methodology tailored to the Bitcoin blockchain and its native currency and aligned with *International Auditing Standards* (ISA). Guided by a pragmatic philosophy and implemented through the design science approach, the book combined insights from literature, empirical validation, and practitioner feedback to design, test, and refine the framework iteratively.

The BTC_AF enables auditors to systematically assess key financial statement assertions and navigate the technical complexities of auditing bitcoin-related balances and transactions, addressing transaction verification, ownership, valuation, and completeness of information. The framework also contributes to audit consistency and stakeholder confidence while supporting auditor training and adaptation to emerging technologies. While the BTC_AF marks a significant advancement, limitations remain regarding tool fragmentation, knowledge requirements, protocol evolution, and its current bitcoin-specific focus.

Keywords Audit profession • Blockchain • Design science • Digital assets • International auditing standards • Financial statement assertions

JEL Classification M15 (IT Management): M42 (Auditing) • O31 (Innovation and Invention) • O33 (Technological Change)

W. Olivier, P. Buys, *Auditing Bitcoin*,
https://doi.org/10.1007/978-981-95-5775-2_9

9.1 Introduction

The previous chapter demonstrated the application of the Bitcoin Audit Framework (BTC_AF), illustrating its practical use. This chapter summarizes the key aspects and outcomes surrounding the BTC_AF development. It begins by revisiting foundational concepts of the Bitcoin protocol's domain, briefly outlines the design philosophy that underpins the design objectives, concludes with an evaluation of the framework's contributions to the audit profession, and acknowledges some limitations.

9.2 Contextual Overview

The integration of blockchain-based digital assets is transforming traditional economic and operational models across various industries (Antonopoulos, 2017), including finance, supply chain, and retail. Evolving from a peer-to-peer (P2P) payment system to a store of value (Nakamoto, 2008), it offers benefits such as increased efficiency, lower transaction costs, and inflation hedging (Dzhereleiko et al., 2023; Hashim et al., 2019). This growing adoption has heightened the need for robust audit frameworks to ensure transparency and reliability in financial reporting in the context of digital assets. The pseudo-anonymous nature of bitcoin, reliance on private key management, and limited third-party verification increase audit complexity and risk (Krimminger et al., 2018). In this context, auditors face significant challenges due to a lack of technical expertise and practical guidance. Without a structured approach, auditors may issue inaccurate opinions, exposing stakeholders to material misstatements.

While blockchain technology's transparency offers an opportunity to gather such evidence, its technical intricacies demand specialized understanding. Auditing transactions executed in bitcoin requires sufficient and reliable evidence aligned with management assertions for balances (existence, completeness, rights and obligations, and valuation) and transactions (occurrence, completeness, accuracy, and cut-off). This book addresses the knowledge gap by developing a structured audit framework, i.e., the BTC_AF, that guides auditors in meeting *International Standards on Auditing* (ISA) requirements while navigating the complexities of auditing bitcoin-related balances and transactions. Through this approach, the book aims to enhance audit reliability and contribute to the evolution of assurance practices for blockchain-based digital assets.

9.3 Design Philosophy

This book adopted a pragmatic design philosophy, blending elements of objectivism and subjectivism to address real-world challenges. It strikes a balance between theoretical depth and practical relevance, thus enabling the integration of diverse methods and perspectives. Pragmatism supports the iterative, problem-solving nature of design science, ensuring alignment between the objectives and the practical needs of auditors working with blockchain-based digital assets.

This design process itself followed an ADR/eADR approach, i.e., an iterative framework well-suited to complex problems, as per Mullarkey and Hevner (2018) and Sein et al. (2011). It involved multiple design, testing, and refinement cycles to develop a robust and practical artifact. Drawing from foundational literature and practitioner input, the design process used the BIE phases herein to create and refine BTC_AF. Feedback from two researcher-practitioner teams was central to verifying and validating the framework. Finally, reflection and formalized learning stages analyzed BIE outcomes, integrating feedback and distilling insights to ensure the final BTC_AF was both theoretically sound and practically relevant.

9.4 Book Objectives

The primary objective was to address the critical knowledge gap in obtaining sufficient and reliable audit evidence for bitcoin-related balances and transactions, as a major blockchain-based digital asset. As blockchain technology reshapes traditional financial systems, auditors face new challenges in obtaining sufficient, reliable evidence under the ISA to support management's assertions related to the financial statements. In attaining this objective, a BTC_AF is to help auditors address the unique challenges of auditing *Virtual Asset Service Providers* (VASPs) and non-VASPs that hold or transact in bitcoin. It sought to bridge the gap between existing auditing standards and the technical features of the Bitcoin blockchain by identifying key audit challenges through literature review and practitioner engagement.

In this context, the secondary objectives supported the primary goal by deepening the BTC_AF's scope and ensuring its completeness as follows:

- Integration of blockchain assets: Through a literature review and practitioner insights, the role of bitcoin across various business models, a system of payment, and a store of value, was clarified while highlighting implications for reporting and strategy. The resultant *Digital Asset Audit Schedule* (DaaS) validated the relevance of this matter.
- Regulatory implications: The DaaS and thematic analysis revealed that audit requirements for organizations that transact in bitcoin often stem from broader regulatory contexts. Despite limited legal mandates, stakeholder risk concerns drive demand for audits to ensure transparency and accountability.
- Audit procedures: The BTC_AF outlined detailed, assertion-linked procedures for *Statement of Financial Position* (SoFP) and *Statement of Profit and Loss* (SoPL) items, providing auditors with clear guidance and consistent methodologies supported by both theoretical and practical justifications.
- Impact on audit practice: Practitioner feedback guided the framework's evolution, ensuring it remained aligned with both technological advancements and practical audit needs, thereby collectively strengthening the BTC_AF's relevance and utility in addressing the complexities of auditing bitcoin-related balances and transactions.

9.5 Contribution

This book makes a significant contribution to the auditing field and profession by addressing the complexities of auditing bitcoin-related balances and transactions. As blockchain technology reshapes traditional business models, auditors must adapt their methods to ensure accurate and reliable financial reporting. The BTC_AF developed herein provides a structured and practical framework to meet these evolving demands. Key contributions include the following:

- Grounded in theoretical insight, empirical testing, and practitioner feedback, this research delivers a methodologically sound and practically relevant framework. Leveraging the ADR/eADR methodology, the process followed a structured, iterative approach that ensured the BTC_AF was both theoretically grounded and practically applicable. Practitioner feedback was integrated throughout to address real-world audit challenges effectively. Formalizing these learnings helped distill insights into a structured, repeatable model that serves both as a practical audit tool and a theoretical contribution. The study demonstrates how eADR can successfully bridge theory and practice, advancing audit methodologies for blockchain-based digital assets.

- Its broader impact lies in reinforcing trust, transparency, and accountability within the digital financial ecosystem, positioning the audit profession to navigate blockchain-related complexities with confidence.
- By integrating technological and auditing concepts, the DaaS and the BTC_AF enhance audit quality in engagements involving blockchain-based digital assets. It not only provides immediate solutions for current audit challenges but also supports the long-term advancement of audit methodologies in response to emerging technologies. The BTC_AF also promotes consistency in audit engagements, reducing variation in approaches and reinforcing the reliability of audit outcomes, thereby strengthening the overall integrity of financial reporting.
- The BTC_AF equips auditors to validate management assertions in line with ISA requirements, promoting consistency and reliability. A key practical contribution lies in its ability to help auditors obtain sufficient and reliable audit evidence for bitcoin-related balances and transactions. It addresses the knowledge gap identified in the DaaS by offering tailored procedures aligned with key financial statement assertions, supporting credible and defensible audit opinions.
- From a stakeholder perspective, the framework enhances trust in both the audit profession and the digital asset space. By equipping auditors with the right tools and knowledge, the BTC_AF enhances confidence among investors, regulators, and the public in the financial statements of entities that utilize blockchain-based digital assets.
- Finally, the framework supports auditor education and training. As a foundational resource, it helps build the skills necessary to navigate the technical complexities of the Bitcoin blockchain and its native currency, ensuring the profession remains agile and future-ready.

9.6 Limitations

Notwithstanding the acknowledged contributions, several limitations may persist due to the evolving nature of blockchain technology, regulatory developments, and constraints on audit tools. These include:

- Protocol evolution: Changes to the Bitcoin protocol via BIPs may require updates to the BTC_AF to maintain relevance.
- Bitcoin-specific scope: The framework is tailored for Bitcoin and may not directly apply to other blockchains or tokens; however, its principles provide a foundation for broader adaptation.
- Fragmented tool ecosystem: The BTC_AF relies on multiple tools for data analysis and verification; a unified, comprehensive tool is currently lacking.
- Fraud risk: Collusion between VASPs and non-VASPs, such as the use of shared keys, may misrepresent asset ownership. Audits under ISA are not explicitly designed to detect fraud.
- Regulatory volatility: Changes in regulations may impact the reliability of third-party custodial confirmations and audit procedures.
- Block height vs. timestamp: Aligning blockchain data (block height) with traditional accounting (timestamps) may resolve reporting inconsistencies.
- Specialized knowledge needs: Effective use of the BTC_AF requires a strong understanding of the Bitcoin protocol, highlighting the need for education and training in blockchain-related topics.
- Rapid market and regulatory change: Auditors must stay current with developments to ensure procedures remain practical and relevant.
- Exclusion of presentation/disclosure assertions: These vary by accounting framework and require auditor judgment beyond the BTC_AF's scope.
- Substantive focus only: The BTC_AF does not cover control testing, which is organization-specific. However, substantive testing remains essential and can stand alone.

9.7 Summary

This book tackles a key challenge in the audit profession: obtaining sufficient and reliable audit evidence for bitcoin-related balances and transactions in financial statements. Through the development of the BTC_AF, a structured framework tailored to the Bitcoin blockchain, the book bridges the knowledge gap identified in the DaaS and supports compliance with professional standards. Guided by the eADR methodology, the BTC_AF links audit procedures directly to management assertions, promoting consistency and enhancing the credibility of audit opinions in engagements involving cryptocurrencies, such as bitcoin.

The framework, therefore, contributes to the profession by standardizing audit approaches in a Bitcoin context, fostering trust in financial reporting, and equipping auditors with tools to address blockchain-related complexities. It also enhances stakeholder confidence in entities that hold or transact with digital assets.

Looking ahead, the BTC_AF offers a foundation for further innovation, including adaptation to other blockchains, evolving regulations, and new audit use cases. Overall, it advances audit methodology, reinforces the audit profession's relevance in a digital economy, and sets the stage for continued development in blockchain asset assurance.

References

Antonopoulos, A. M. (2017). *Mastering bitcoin: Programming the open blockchain*. O'Reilly Media.

Dzhereleiko, S., Shevchenko, M. M., & Nazarova, T. Y. (2023). *Development of financial services based on cryptocurrencies*. https://repository.kpi.kharkov.ua/handle/KhPI-Press/71817

Hashim, M. J., Kamarudin, M. F., Muhamad Arifin, N. A., & Khamis, M. R. (2019). Customer benefits on bitcoin as a medium of exchange. *Advances in Business Research International Journal, 5*(1), 22–30.

Krimminger, M. H., Lloyd, C., Rocks, S., Steen, C. G., & Hamilton, L. L. P. (2018). Custody and transfer of digital assets: Key US legal considerations. In J. Dewey (Ed.), *Blockchain & cryptocurrency regulation* (pp. 121–131). Global Legal Group.

Mullarkey, M. T., & Hevner, A. R. (2018). An elaborated action design research process model. *European Journal of Information Systems, 28*(1), 6–20.

Nakamoto, S. (2008). *Bitcoin: A peer-to-peer electronic cash system*. https://assets.pubpub.org/d8wct41f/31611263538139.pdf

Sein, M. K., Henfridsson, O., Purao, S., Rossi, M., & Lindgren, R. (2011). Action design research. *MIS Quarterly*, 37–56.

Index[1]

[1] Note: Page numbers followed by 'n' refer to notes.

W. Olivier, P. Buys, *Auditing Bitcoin*,
https://doi.org/10.1007/978-981-95-5775-2